CONTEN

QUOTATIONS
with an
Attitude

A
WICKEDLY
FUNNY
SOURCE
BOOK

ROY L. STEWART

Sterling Publishing Co., Inc.   New York

This book is dedicated with love and respect to Mary Dondanville.
Everyone should have such a friend.

ACKNOWLEDGMENTS

The errors are mine, but much of the credit lies with the following:
Richard Ferris, Joy Barto, Carol Clare, Allen Stewart, Jennifer
Watkins, Janice DeLuzio, Wendy Edwards, De Hermanson, John and
Carol Sherman, Anna Greene, and Carol Musser for general encouragement.

Library of Congress Cataloging-in Publication Data

Stewart, Roy L.
    Quotations with an attitude : a wickedly funny source
book / by Roy L. Stewart.
        p.   cm.
    Includes index.
    ISBN 0-8069-0966-8
    1. Quotations, English. I. Title
PN6081.S735 1995
082–c20   94—4560
                                                       CIP

10 9 8 7 6 5 4 3 2 1

Published by Sterling Publishing Company, Inc.
387 Park Avenue South, New York, N.Y. 10016
©1995 by Roy L. Stewart
Distributed in Canada by Sterling Publishing
c/o Canadian Manda Group, One Atlantic Avenue, Suite 105
Toronto, Ontario, Canada M6K 3E7
Distributed in Great Britain and Europe by Cassell PLC
Wellington House, 125 Strand, London WC2R 0BB, England
Distributed in Australia by Capricorn Link (Australia) Pty Ltd.
P.O. Box 6651, Baulkham Hills, Business Centre, NSW 2153, Australia
Manufactured in the United States of America
All rights reserved
Sterling ISBN 0-8069-0966-8

THE HUMAN ANIMAL

To err is human; to forgive, infrequent.
—Franklin P. Adams
(1881-1960)

In each human heart is a tiger, a pig, an ass and a nightingale. Diversity of character is due to their unequal activity.
—Ambrose Bierce
(1842-1914)

More than any time in history mankind faces a crossroads. One path leads to despair and utter hopelessness; the other to total extinction. Let us pray that we have the wisdom to choose correctly.
—Woody Allen

The world's a stage and most of us are desperately unrehearsed.
—Sean O'Casey

It is absurd to divide people into good and bad. People are either charming or tedious.
—Oscar Wilde
(1854-1900)

The chief obstacle to the progress of the human race is the human race.
—Don Marquis
(1879-1937)

BIRTH & CHILDHOOD

When I was born I was so surprised I didn't talk for a year and a half.
—Gracie Allen
(1906–1964)

Everyone is born with genius, but most people only keep it a few minutes.
—Edgard Varèse

I was born in Australia because my mother wanted me to be near her.
—Anonymous

You should have thought of all this before you were born.
—N.F. Simpson

To my embarrassment I was born in bed with a lady.
—Wilson Mizner

My obstetrician was so dumb that when I gave birth he forgot to cut the cord. For a year that kid followed me everywhere. It was like having a dog on a leash. —*Joan Rivers*

We are all born charming, fresh and spontaneous and must be civilized before we are fit to participate in society. —*Judith Martin ("Miss Manners")*

Giving birth is like trying to push a piano through a transom. —*Alice Roosevelt Longworth (1884–1980)*

The baby was so ugly they had to hang a pork chop around its neck to get the dog to play with it. —*Anonymous*

My mother didn't breast-feed me. She said she liked me as a friend. —*Rodney Dangerfield*

An ugly baby is a very nasty object, and the prettiest is frightful when undressed. —*Queen Victoria (1819–1901)*

Babies don't need vacations, but I still see them at the beach. —*Steven Wright*

I have been assured by a very knowing American of acquaintance in London, that a young healthy child well nursed is, at a year old, a most delicious, nourishing and wholesome food, whether stewed, roasted, baked or boiled, and I make no doubt that it will equally serve in a fricassee or a ragout. —*Jonathan Swift*

A child is a curly, dimpled lunatic. —*Ralph Waldo Emerson (1803–1882)*

As for children, I keep as far from them as possible. I don't like the sight of them. The scale is all wrong. The heads tend to be too big for the bodies, and the hands and feet are a disaster. They should be neither seen nor heard, and no one must make another one.
—*Gore Vidal*

Children today are tyrants. They contradict their parents, gobble their food and tyrannize their teachers. —*Socrates (470–399 B.C.)*

I love children, especially when they cry, for then someone takes them away. —*Nancy Mitford*

Learning to dislike children at an early age saves a lot of expense and aggravation later in life. —*Robert Byrne*

All God's children are not beautiful. Most of God's children are, in fact, barely presentable. —*Fran Lebowitz*

Providence protects children and idiots. I know because I have tested it. —*Mark Twain*

The highlight of my childhood was making my brother laugh so hard that food came out of his nose. —*Garrison Keillor*

We had a quicksand box in our backyard. I was an only child, eventually. —*Steven Wright*

A child is a person who can't understand why someone would give away a perfectly good kitten. —*Doug Larson*

Every child is an artist. The problem is how to remain an artist once he grows up. —*Pablo Picasso*

People who get nostalgic about childhood were obviously never children. —*Bill Watterson*
"Calvin and Hobbes"

All children are essentially criminal. —*Denis Diderot*
(1713–1784)

The persons hardest to convince they're at the retirement age are children at bedtime. —*Shannon Fife*

A characteristic of the normal child is he doesn't act that way very often. —*Laurence J. Peter*

I was the kid next door's imaginary friend. —*Emo Phillips*

If a child shows himself to be incorrigible, he should be decently and quietly beheaded at the age of twelve lest he grow to maturity, marry and perpetuate his kind. —*Don Marquis*
(1878–1937)

There was a time when we expected nothing of children but obedience, as opposed to the present, when we expect everything of them but obedience. —*Anatole Broyard*

Children of the poor should work for some part of the day when they reach the age of three. —*John Locke*
(1632–1704)

Of all the animals, the boy is the most unmanageable. —*Plato*
(427?–348? B.C.)

Nature makes boys and girls lovely to look at so they can be tolerated until they acquire some sense. —*William Lyon Phelps*
(1865–1943)

Blessed are the young, for they shall inherit the national debt.
—*Herbert Hoover*
(1874–1964)

When you are eight years old, nothing is any of your business.
—*Lenny Bruce*

I was so naive as a kid I used to sneak behind the barn and do nothing. —*Johnny Carson*

In America there are two classes of travel—first class, and with children. —*Robert Benchley*

I know a little boy who told me . . . he could easily have won a race at his school except there was another boy who ran faster.
—*Stephen Leacock*

You can't expect a boy to be depraved until he has been to a good school. —*H.H. Munro*
("Saki")

Everyone is in awe of the lion tamer in a cage with half a dozen lions—everyone but a school bus driver. —*Laurence J. Peter*

Give a small boy a hammer and he will find that everything he encounters needs pounding. —*Abraham Kaplan*

There are three terrible ages of childhood—1 to 10, 10 to 20 and 20 to 30. —*Cleveland Amory*

YOUTH

Adolescence is the stage between infancy and adultery.
—*Anonymous*

God's way of making separation with children easier was to invent adolescence. —*Mark Patinkin*

There's nothing wrong with teenagers that reasoning with them won't aggravate. —*Anonymous*

If Abraham's son had been a teenager, it wouldn't have been a sacrifice.   —*Scott Spendlove*

Like its politicians and its wars, society has the teenagers it deserves.
                                                                        —*J.B. Priestley*

The denunciation of the young is a necessary part of the hygiene of older people, and greatly assists in the circulation of the blood.
                                                                        —*Logan Pearsall Smith*
                                                                        (1865–1946)

One good thing about being young is that you are not experienced enough to know you cannot possibly do the things you are doing.
                                                                        —*Gene Brown*

If you want to recapture your youth, cut off his allowance.
                                                                        —*Al Bernstein*

What is youth except a man or a woman before it is ready or fit to be seen?   —*Evelyn Waugh*

A recent survey finds that 15- to 19-year-olds now have fewer sexual partners than they did ten years ago.
                                                                        —*Radio Station WEEI—Boston*

Young men are apt to think themselves wise enough, as drunken men are to think themselves sober enough.   —*Earl of Chesterfield*

Young men are fitter to invent than to judge, fitter for execution than for counsel, fitter for new projects than settled business.
                                                                        —*Francis Bacon*

A young man with good health and a poor appetite can save up money.   —*James Montgomery Bailey*

Youth is such a wonderful thing. What a crime to waste it on children.   —*George Bernard Shaw*

PARENTHOOD

My father was frightened of his father, I was frightened of my father and I am damned well going to see to it that my children are frightened of me.   —*King George V*
                                                                        (1865–1936)

9

The time not to become a father is eighteen years before a war.
—*E.B. White*
(1899–1985)

To be a successful father, there is one absolute rule: When you have a kid, don't look at it for the first two years.   —*Ernest Hemingway*

When asked why he did not become a father, Thales answered, "Because I am fond of children."   —*Diogenes Laertius*
(c.150 B.C.)

It's a dull child that knows less than its father.   —*Anonymous*

A father is a man who expects his son to be as good a man as he meant to be.   —*Frank A. Clark*

I phoned my dad to tell him I had stopped smoking. He called me a quitter.   —*Steven Pearl*

When I meet a man I ask myself, "Is this the man I want my children to spend their weekends with?"   —*Rita Rudner*

My mom was fair. You never knew whether she was going to swing with her right or her left.   —*Herb Caen*

As a housewife, I feel that if the kids are still alive when my husband gets home from work, then, hey, I've done my job.   —*Roseanne*

A suburban mother's role is to deliver children obstetrically once, and by car forever after.   —*Peter De Vries*

Mothers are fonder than fathers of their children because they are more certain they are their own.   —*Aristotle*

No matter how old a mother is, she watches her middle-aged chilren for signs of improvement.   —*Florida Scott-Maxwell*

My mother loved children—she would have given anything if I had been one.   —*Groucho Marx*

Reinhart was never his mother's favorite—and he was an only child.
—*Thomas Berger*

Conscience: That which makes a boy tell his mother before his sister does.   —*Laurence J. Peter*

Cleaning your house while your kids are still growing is like shoveling the walk before it stops snowing.   —*Phyllis Diller*

I could now afford all the things I never had as a kid, if I didn't have kids.
—*Robert Orben*

I take my children everywhere, but they always find their way back home.
—*Robert Orben*

Never lend your car to anyone to whom you have given birth.
—*Erma Bombeck*

The best revenge is to live long enough to be a problem to your children.
—*Anonymous*

I'm not going to buy my kids an encyclopedia. Let them walk to school like I did.
—*Anonymous*

When childhood dies, its corpses are called adults. —*Brian Aldiss*

Adults are obsolete children.
—*Dr. Seuss*

Thanksgiving comes after Christmas for people over thirty.
—*Peter Kreeft*

Setting a good example for children takes all the fun out of middle age.
—*William Feather*

There is no such thing as "fun for the whole family."
—*Jerry Seinfeld*

My parents only had one argument in forty-five years. It lasted forty-three years.
—*Cathy Ladman*

When I was kidnapped, my parents snapped into action. They rented out my room.
—*Woody Allen*

The first half of our lives is ruined by our parents and the second half by our children.
—*Clarence Darrow*
(1857–1938)

As parents, my wife and I have one thing in common. We're both afraid of children.
—*Bill Cosby*

Ask your child what he wants for dinner only if he's buying.
—*Fran Lebowitz*

My parents were too poor to have children, so the neighbors had me.
—*Buddy Hackett*

Have children while your parents are still young enough to take care of them.
—*Rita Rudner*

Parenthood remains the greatest single preserve of the amateur.
—Alvin Toffler

Parents are not interested in justice, they are interested in quiet.
—Bill Cosby

My parents have been visiting me for a few days. I just dropped them off at the airport. They leave tomorrow. *—Margaret Smith*

Parents are the bones on which children cut their teeth.
—Peter Ustinov

A parent's job is eventually to be out of a job. *—Denise Topolnick*

If you don't want your children to hear what you are saying, pretend you're talking to them. *—Anonymous*

You can learn many things from children. How much patience you have, for instance. *—Franklin P. Adams*
(1881-1960)

The modern child will answer you back before you've said anything.
—Laurence J. Peter

People who say they sleep like a baby usually don't have one.
—Leo J. Burke

Before I was married I had three theories about raising children. Now I have three children and no theories. *—John Wilmot*
Earl of Rochester
(1647–1680)

Before I got married I had six theories about bringing up children; now I have six children and no theories. *—John Wilmot*
Earl of Rochester
(1647–1680)

The thing that impresses me most about America is the way parents obey their children. *—Duke of Windsor*
(Edward VIII)

You know that children are growing up when they start asking questions that have answers. *—John J. Plomp*

Parents are the last people on earth who ought to have children.
—Samuel Butler

The secret of dealing successfully with a child is not to be its parent.
—*Mell Lazarus*

Every child should have an occasional pat on the back as long as it is applied low enough and hard enough.   —*Bishop Fulton J. Sheen*

Likely as not, the child you can do the least with will do the most to make you proud.   —*Mignon McLaughlin*

If your parents didn't have any children, there's a good chance that you won't have any.   —*Clarence Day*

No man knows his true character until he has run out of gas, purchased something on the installment plan and raised an adolescent.
—*Mercelene Cox*

I have never understood the fear of some parents about babies getting mixed up in the hospital. What difference does it make as long as you get a good one?   —*Heywood Broun*
(1888–1939)

Never raise your hand to your children—it leaves your midsection unprotected.   —*Robert Orben*

One of the disadvantages of having children is that they eventually get old enough to give you the presents they make at school.
—*Robert Byrne*

I can't believe I forgot to have children!   —*Anonymous*

My parents put a live teddy bear in my crib.   —*Woody Allen*

I'd get pregnant if I could be assured I'd have puppies.
—*Cynthia Nelms*

When my kids become wild and unruly, I use a nice, safe playpen. When they're finished, I climb out.   —*Erma Bombeck*

The best way to keep children home is to make the home atmosphere pleasant—and let the air out of the tires.   —*Dorothy Parker*

Children are unpredictable. You never know what inconsistency they're going to catch you in next.   —*Franklin P. Adams*
(1881-1960)

The reason grandparents and grandchildren get along so well is that they have a common enemy.   —*Sam Levenson*
(1911–1980)

In order to influence a child, one must be careful not to be that child's parent or grandparent.
—*Don Marquis*
(1878-1937)

By the time the youngest children have learned to keep the house tidy, the oldest grandchildren are on hand to tear it to pieces.
—*Christopher Morley*

Never have children, only grandchildren.
—*Gore Vidal*

ADULTHOOD & MIDDLE AGE

Middle age begins with the first mortgage and ends when you drop dead.
—*Herb Caen*

One good thing about middle-age spread is that it brings people closer together.
—*Martin Buxbaum*

Middle age is when you've met so many people that every new person you meet reminds you of someone else.
—*Ogden Nash*
(1902-1971)

Thirty-five is a very attractive age. London's society is full of women who have, of their free choice, remained thirty-five for years.
—*Oscar Wilde*
(1854-1900)

My notion of a wife at forty is that a man should be able to change her, like a bank note, for two twenties.
—*Douglas Jerrold*

The best years are the forties; after fifty a man begins to deteriorate, but in the forties he is at the maximum of his villainy.
—*H.L. Mencken*
(1880-1956)

The years between 50 and 70 are the hardest. You are always asked to do things, and you are not yet decrepit enough to turn them down.
—*T.S. Eliot*

OLD AGE

I lived in Miami for a while, in a section with a lot of really old people. The average age in my apartment house was dead.
—*Gabe Kaplan*

I have an aunt who married so late in life that Medicare picked up 80 percent of the honeymoon.   —*Don Reber*

On the lighter side of the news: A couple celebrating their 90th wedding anniversary died of shock today at the beginning of a surprise party.   —*George Carlin*

If you live to the age of a hundred you have it made because very few people die past the age of a hundred.   —*George Burns*

Retirement at sixty-five is ridiculous. When I was sixty-five I still had pimples.   —*George Burns*

If you live long enough, the venerability factor creeps in; first, you get accused of things you never did, and later, credited for virtues you never had.   —*I.F. Stone*

If you survive long enough, you're revered—rather like an old building.   —*Katharine Hepburn*

I should have been a country-western singer. After all, I'm older than most western countries.   —*George Burns*

You'll know you're old when everything hurts and what doesn't hurt doesn't work.   —*George Burns*

It takes about ten years to get used to how old you are.   —*Anonymous*

Just remember: When you're over the hill you begin to pick up speed.   —*Charles M. Schulz*

To me, old age is fifteen years older than I am.   —*Bernard M. Baruch*

I'll never make the mistake of bein' seventy again!   —*Casey Stengel*

I stay away from natural foods. At my age I need all the preservatives I can get.   —*George Burns*

I'm at the age where every time I see a girl I used to know, it's her daughter.   —*Earl Wilson*

The older they get the better they were when they were younger.   —*Jim Bouton*

You're never too old to become younger.   —*Mae West*

The secret of staying young is to live honestly, eat slowly and lie about your age.
—*Lucille Ball*

I am in the prime of senility.
—*Joel Chandler Harris*
(1848–1908)

I am not young enough to know everything.
—*Oscar Wilde*
(1854-1900)

Old age is when the liver spots show through your gloves.
—*Phyllis Diller*

Old age is like a plane flying through a storm. Once you are aboard there is nothing you can do.
—*Golda Meir*
(1898–1978)

You know you're old when you notice how young the derelicts are getting.
—*Jeanne Phillips*

You have to be an antique to appreciate them.
—*Fay Madigan Lange*

You don't stop laughing because you grow old. You grow old because you stop laughing.
—*Michael Pritchard*

Old age comes at a bad time.
—*Sue Banducci*

After a certain age, if you don't wake up aching in every joint, you are probably dead.
—*Tommy Mein*

You know you're getting old when you stoop to tie your shoes and wonder what else you can do while you're down there.
—*George Burns*

Old age means realizing you will never own all the dogs you wanted to.
—*Joe Gores*

Children are a great comfort in your old age—and they help you reach it faster, too.
—*Lionel Kauffman*

My grandmother started walking five miles a day when she was sixty. She's ninety-seven now, and we don't know where the hell she is.
—*Ellen DeGeneris*

When I was young, the Dead Sea was still alive.
—*George Burns*

My health is good; it's my age that's bad.
—*Roy Acuff*
(At age 83)

A friend of mine was asked how she liked having her first great-grandchild. "It was wonderful," she replied, "until I suddenly realized that I was the mother of a grandfather!" —*Robert L. Rice, M.D.*

The older a man grows, the faster he could run as a boy.
—*Red Smith*

You lose a lot of speed between 80 and 86. —*Ruth Rothfarb, 86*
(On not improving her
personal best in the marathon)

The older I grow, the more I distrust the familiar doctrine that age brings wisdom. —*H.L. Mencken*
(1880-1956)

Old people love to give good advice; it compensates them for their inability to set a bad example. —*Duc de La Rochefoucauld*
(1613–1680)

For certain people, after fifty, litigation takes the place of sex.
—*Gore Vidal*

One should never make one's debut in a scandal. One should reserve that to give interest to one's old age. —*Oscar Wilde*
(1854-1900)

When you're through changing, you're through. —*Bruce Barton*

By the time we've made it, we've had it. —*Malcolm Forbes*

There was no respect for youth when I was young, and now that I am old, there is no respect for age. I missed it coming and going.
—*J.B. Priestley*

The hardest years in life are those between ten and seventy.
—*Helen Hayes*
(At age 83)

LOVE

If you want to read about love and marriage, you've got to buy two separate books. —*Alan King*

No matter how much cats fight, there always seem to be plenty of kittens. —*Abraham Lincoln*
(1809–1865)

Love is the delusion that one woman differs from another.
>—*H.L. Mencken*
>*(1880-1956)*

Love is an obsessive delusion that is cured by marriage.
>—*Dr. Karl Bowman*
>*(1888–1973)*

You need someone to love while you're looking for someone to love.
>—*Shelagh Delaney*

Spring is when a boy mantis sees a girl mantis and finally realizes what he's been praying for.
>—*Robert Orben*

People who are sensible about love are incapable of it.
>—*Douglas Yates*

Of course there is such a thing as love, or there wouldn't be so many divorces.
>—*Ed Howe*

Only little boys and old men sneer at love.
>—*Louis Auchincloss*

Send two dozen roses to room 424 and put "Emily, I love you" on the back of the bill.
>—*Groucho Marx*

Love is an ocean of emotions surrounded by expenses.
>—*Lord Dewar*

In expressing love we belong among the undeveloped countries.
>—*Saul Bellow*

A man can be happy with any woman as long as he does not love her.
>—*Oscar Wilde*
>*(1854-1900)*

If I love you, what business is it of yours?
>—*Johann von Goethe*
>*(1749–1832)*

The perfect lover is one who turns into a pizza at 4:00 A.M.
>—*Charles Pierce*

Love is the crocodile on the river of desire.
>—*Bhartrihari*
>*(c.625)*

Love is what happens to men and women who don't know each other.
>—*W. Somerset Maugham*
>*(1874–1965)*

Emily, will you marry me? I will never look at another horse.
—*Groucho Marx*

The trouble with loving is that pets don't last long enough and people last too long. —*Anonymous*

Better to have loved and lost a short person than never to have loved a tall. —*David Chambless*

One of the advantages of living alone is that you don't have to wake up in the arms of a loved one. —*Marion Smith*

There is no love sincerer than the love of food.
—*George Bernard Shaw*

Momma? Oedipus Schmedipus. I love you. —*Robin Williams*

Love your enemies in case your friends turn out to be a bunch of bastards. —*R.A. Dickson*

I hate people. People make me pro-nuclear. —*Margaret Smith*

Love is an exploding cigar we willingly smoke. —*Lynda Barry*

The difference between sex and love is that sex relieves tension and love causes it. —*Woody Allen*

It's silly to go on pretending that under the skin we are all brothers. The truth is more likely that under the skin we are all cannibals, assassins, traitors, liars, hypocrites, poltroons. —*Henry Miller*

That all men should be brothers is the dream of people who have no brothers. —*Charles Chincholles*

Always forgive your enemies—nothing annoys them so much.
—*Oscar Wilde*
(1854-1900)

One should forgive one's enemies, but not before they are hanged.
—*Heinrich Heine*

I like long walks, especially when they are taken by people who annoy me. —*Noël Coward*

People who never get carried away should be. —*Malcolm S. Forbes*

I hope that while so many people are out smelling the flowers, someone is taking the time to plant some. —*Herbert Rappaport*

Love is the triumph of imagination over intelligence.
> —*H.L. Mencken*
> *(1880-1956)*

Gravitation cannot be held responsible for people falling in love.
> —*Albert Einstein*

Love is the delightful interval between meeting a beautiful girl and discovering that she looks like a haddock.
> —*John Barrymore*
> *(1882–1942)*

Beauty is only skin deep, and the world is full of thin-skinned people.
> —*Richard Armour*

Beauty and folly are generally companions.
> —*Baltasar Gracian*
> *(1601–1658)*

A beautiful woman is the hell of the soul, the purgatory of the purse, and the paradise of the eyes.
> —*Fontenelle*

I know that there are people who do not love their fellow man, and I hate people like that!
> —*Tom Lehrer*

Love cures people; both the ones who give it, and the ones who receive it.
> —*Dr. Karl Menninger*

I never hated a man enough to give him his diamonds back.
> —*Zsa Zsa Gabor*

Many a man has fallen in love with a girl in a light so dim he would not have chosen a suit by it.
> —*Maurice Chevalier*

It is better to have loved and lost than to do forty pounds of laundry a week.
> —*Laurence J. Peter*

Love is a dirty trick played on us to achieve the continuation of the species.
> —*W. Somerset Maugham*
> *(1874-1965)*

LIFE & EXPERIENCE

They lived and laughed and loved and left.
> —*James Joyce*
> Finnegans Wake

Good judgment comes from experience, which comes from poor judgment.
> —*Anonymous*

It's a dog-eat-dog world, and I'm wearing Milk Bone shorts.
—Kelly Allen

There are days when it takes all you've got just to keep up with the losers.
—Robert Orben

When you don't have any money, the problem is food. When you have money, it's sex. When you have both, it's health. If everything is simply jake, then you're frightened of death.
—J.P. Donleavy

I have found little that is good about human beings. In my experience most of them are trash.
—Sigmund Freud
(1856–1939)

Life is like playing a violin in public and learning the instrument as one goes on.
—Samuel Butler
(1835–1902)

There may come a time when the lion and the lamb will lie down together, but I am still betting on the lion.
—Henry Wheeler Shaw

It may be that the race is not always to the swift, nor the battle to the strong—but that is the way to bet.
—Damon Runyon

Literature is mostly about having sex and not much about having children. Life is the other way around.
—David Lodge

If you look good and dress well, you don't need a purpose in life.
—Robert Pante

The trouble with life in the fast lane is that you get to the other end in an awful hurry.
—John Jensen

If you can see the light at the end of the tunnel you are looking the wrong way.
—Barry Commoner

We're all in this alone.
—Lily Tomlin

A life spent making mistakes is not only more honorable but more useful than a life spent doing nothing.
—George Bernard Shaw

Start every day off with a smile and get it over with.
—W.C. Fields

Life is divided into the horrible and the miserable.
—Woody Allen

Life being what it is, one dreams of revenge.
—Paul Gauguin
(1848–1903)

If I had my life to live over, I'd live it over a delicatessen.

—Anonymous

Some mornings it just doesn't seem worth it to gnaw through the leather straps. *—Emo Phillips*

Everything I did in my life that was worthwhile I caught hell for.

—Chief Justice Earl Warren
(1891–1974)

There are few problems in life that wouldn't be eased by the proper application of high explosives. *—Anonymous*

You've got to take the bitter with the sour. *—Samuel Goldwyn*

Success has many fathers. Failure is a mother. *—Jeanne Phillips*

If at first you don't succeed, find out if the loser gets anything.

—Bill Lyon

Success in life means not becoming like your parents.

—Louise Bowie

Mondays are the potholes in the road of life. *—Tom Wilson*

Some people are born on third base and go through life thinking they hit a triple. *—Barry Switzer*

Life is a fragile bargain, rescindable at any time by the other party.

—Joseph Epstein

Life is what you make it; if you snooze, you lose and if you snore, you lose more. *—Phyllis George*

I like life. It's something to do. *—Ronnie Shakes*

The examined life is no picnic. *—Robert Fulghum*

Life is far too important a thing ever to talk seriously about.

—Oscar Wilde
(1854-1900)

If people concentrated on the really important things in life, there'd be a shortage of fishing poles. *—Doug Larson*

Why is life so tough? Perhaps it was cooked too long.

—University of North Carolina-Charlotte
Philosophy Department

There are two tragedies in life. One is to lose your heart's desire; the other is to gain it. —*George Bernard Shaw*

80% of life is just showing up. —*Woody Allen*

I think that somehow, we learn who we really are and then live with that decision. —*Eleanor Roosevelt*

We all learn by experience but some of us have to go to summer school. —*Peter De Vries*

There is nothing new under the sun but there are lots of old things we don't know. —*Ambrose Bierce*
(1842-1914)

Use your health, even to the point of wearing it out. That is what it is for. Spend all you have before you die, and do not outlive yourself.
—*George Bernard Shaw*

We are continually faced with a series of great opportunities brilliantly disguised as insoluble problems. —*John W. Gardner*

We are what we pretend to be. —*Kurt Vonnegut, Jr.*

We think in generalities, but we live in detail.
—*Alfred North Whitehead*
(1861–1947)

The optimist proclaims that we live in the best of all possible worlds, and the pessimist fears that this is true. —*James Branch Cabell*

Laughing at ourselves is possible when we are able to see humanity as it is—a little lower than the angels and at times only slightly higher than the apes. —*Tom Mullen*

If you think nobody cares if you're alive, try missing a couple of car payments. —*Earl Wilson*

If you want a place in the sun, you've got to expect a few blisters.
—*Abigail Van Buren*
("Dear Abby")

Life is an unbroken succession of false situations.
—*Thornton Wilder*
(1897–1975)

My life has a superb cast but I can't figure out the plot.
—*Ashleigh Brilliant*

No man remains quite what he was when he recognizes himself.
—Thomas Mann
(1875–1955)

The greatest use of life is to spend it for something that will outlast it.
—William James

All you need in this life is ignorance and confidence, and then success is sure.
—Mark Twain

As you ramble on through life, brother, whatever be your goal: Keep you eyes upon the donut, and not upon the hole!
—Dr. Murray Banks

Experience is the hardest kind of teacher. It gives you the test first, and the lesson afterward.
—Anonymous

Figure it out. Work a lifetime to pay off a house. You finally own it and there's no one to live in it.
—Arthur Miller
Death of a Salesman

Give me the luxuries of life and I will willingly do without the necessities.
—Frank Lloyd Wright

Half a man's life is devoted to what he calls improvements, yet the original had some quality which is lost in the process.
—E.B. White
(1899–1985)

I predict that exact reproduction through cloning will not become popular. Too many people already find it difficult to live with themselves.
—Jeanne Dixon

As to posterity, I may ask what has it ever done for us?
—Thomas Gray
(1716–1771)

My grandfather always said that living is like licking honey off a thorn.
—Louis Adamic

Let us endeavor so to live that when we come to die even the undertaker will be sorry.
—Mark Twain

In spite of the cost of living, it's still popular.   *—Laurence J. Peter*

We are all here for a spell; get all the good laughs you can.
—Will Rogers

Whatever you do, you'll regret it.   *—Allan McLeod Gray*

Seeing ourselves as others see us would probably confirm our worst suspicions about them. —*Franklin P. Adams*
(1881-1960)

Life isn't fair. It's just fairer than death, that's all.
—*William Goldman*
The Princess Bride

The world is a stage, but the play is badly cast. —*Oscar Wilde*
(1854-1900)

Life is nothing but a competition to be the criminal rather than the victim. —*Bertrand Russell*

The golden rule is that there are no golden rules.
—*George Bernard Shaw*
(1856-1950)

The very purpose of existence is to reconcile the glowing opinion we hold of ourselves with the appalling things that other people think about us. —*Quentin Crisp*

There is no cure for birth or death except to try and enjoy the interval. —*George Santayana*
(1863–1952)

My interest is in the future, because I'm going to spend the rest of my life there. —*Charles Kettering*

It was always thus; and even if 'twere not, 'twould inevitably have been always thus. —*Dean Lattimer*

The shortest distance between two points is under construction.
—*Noélie Altito*

The trouble with our times is that the future is not what it used to be.
—*Paul Valéry*

You can't have everything. Where would you put it? —*Steven Wright*

Nostalgia is the realization that things weren't as unbearable as they seemed at the time. —*Anonymous*

The fixity of a habit is generally in direct proportion to its absurdity.
—*Marcel Proust*

The man who says he is willing to meet you halfway is usually a poor judge of distance. —*Laurence J. Peter*

25

Getting out of bed in the morning is an act of false confidence.
—*Jules Feiffer*

We learn from experience that men never learn anything from experience.
—*George Bernard Shaw*
(1856-1950)

No good deed goes unpunished.
—*Clare Boothe Luce*

It has been observed that one's nose is never so happy as when it is thrust into the affairs of another, from which some physiologists have drawn the inference that the nose is devoid of the sense of smell.
—*Ambrose Bierce*
(1842-1914)

DEATH

For three days after death, hair and fingernails continue to grow, but phone calls taper off.
—*Johnny Carson*

I don't have a warm personal enemy left. They've all died off. I miss them terribly because they helped define me.
—*Clare Boothe Luce*

I'm lonesome. They are all dying. I have hardly a warm personal enemy left.
—*James McNeill Whistler*
(1834–1903)

Some people are always late, like the late King George V.
—*Spike Milligan*

> Early to rise,
> Early to bed,
> Makes a man healthy,
> Wealthy, and dead.
—*James Thurber*

Exercise daily. Eat wisely. Die anyway.
—*Anonymous*

On CBS Radio the news of his [Ed Murrow's] death, reportedly from lung cancer, was followed by a cigarette commercial.
—*Alexander Kendrick*

I don't believe in dying. It's been done. I'm working on a new exit. Besides, I can't die now. I'm booked.
—*George Burns*

Dying is one of the few things that can be done as easily lying down.
—*Woody Allen*

I'm not afraid to die; I just don't want to be there when it happens.
—*Woody Allen*

There is no such thing as inner peace. There is only nervousness
and death. —*Fran Lebowitz*

The graveyards are full of indispensable men. —*Charles de Gaulle*
(1890–1970)

Defeat is worse than death because you have to live with defeat.
—*Bill Musselman*

Death is just a distant rumor to the young. —*Andy Rooney*

There is no reason for me to die. I already died in Altoona.
—*George Burns*

Death sneaks up on you like a windshield sneaks up on a bug.
—*Anonymous*

Errol Flynn died on a seventy-foot yacht with a seventeen-year-old
girl. Walter's always wanted to go that way, but he's going to settle
for a seventeen-footer and a seventy-year-old.
—*Mrs. Walter Cronkite*

I don't want to achieve immortality by being inducted into baseball's
Hall of Fame. I want to achieve immortality by not dying.
—*Leo Durocher*
(At age 81)

I don't want to achieve immortality through my work. I want to
achieve it through not dying. —*Woody Allen*

It was a struggle and the gun went off. I didn't want to kill him. I
wouldn't do that at my Dad's house. I'd take him down the road.
—*Christian Brando*
(Sentenced to 10 years for killing his sister's boyfriend
at this father [Marlon]'s estate)

We wish more [young veterans] would join because the rest of us are
about ready to die. —*Paul Zimmer*
(Chaplain of Myrtle Beach, S.C., VFW Post, speaking about
its membership drive.)

I know a man who gave up smoking, drinking, sex and rich food. He
was healthy right up to the time he killed himself. —*Johnny Carson*

Suicide is cheating the doctors out of a job. —*Josh Billings*

27

The man who, in a fit of melancholy, kills himself today, would have wished to live had he waited a week.   —*Voltaire*

Suicide is belated acquiescence in the opinion of one's wife's relatives.   —*H.L. Mencken*
                                                                    (1880-1956)

Those who welcome death have only tried it from the ears up.
                                                              —*Wilson Mizner*

Every man of genius is considerably helped by being dead.
                                                              —*Robert S. Lynd*

He is one of those people who would be enormously improved by death.   —*H.H. Munro*
                                                                      ("Saki")

To be seen is the ambition of ghosts, and to be remembered is the ambition of the dead.   —*Norman O. Brown*

My goal is to die young at a very old age.   —*Anonymous*

The only thing wrong with immortality is that it tends to go on forever.   —*Herb Caen*

Luck can't last a lifetime unless you die young.   —*Russell Banks*

Time is a great teacher, but unfortunately it kills all its pupils.
                                                              —*Hector Berlioz*

We hold these truths to be self-evident: all men could be cremated equal.   —*Vern Parlow*

We seem to believe it is possible to ward off death by following rules of good grooming.   —*Don Delillo*

Why shouldn't things be largely absurd, futile and transitory? They are so, and we are so, and they and we go very well together.
                                                            —*George Santayana*

I didn't know he was dead; I thought he was British.   —*Anonymous*

Either this man is dead or my watch has stopped.   —*Groucho Marx*

If death did not exist today it would be necessary to invent it.
                                                  —*Count Jean Baptiste Milhoud*

Is there life before death?   —*Belfast graffito*

It is impossible to experience one's death objectively and still carry a tune. —*Woody Allen*

No, 'tis not so deep as a well, nor so wide as a church-door; but 'tis enough, 'twill serve . . . —*William Shakespeare*
(1564-1616)
Mercutio
Romeo & Juliet

Often it is fatal to live too long. —*Racine*

Our existence is but a brief crack of light between two eternities of darkness. —*Vladimir Nabokov*

A single death is a tragedy; a million deaths is a statistic. —*Joseph Stalin*

Death meant little to me. It was the last joke in a series of bad jokes. —*Charles Bukowski*

The good die young. They see it's no use living if you've got to be good. —*John Barrymore*

Pathologist—One who carves a good living out of a bad death. —*Gordon Bowker*

I get my exercise acting as a pallbearer to my friends who exercise. —*Chauncey Depew*
(1834–1928)

The only exercise I get is as pallbearer for my friends who exercise. —*Red Skelton*

Memorial Service—Farewell party for someone who has already left. —*Robert Byrne*

They say such nice things about people at their funerals that it makes me sad to realize that I'm going to miss mine by just a few days. —*Garrison Keillor*

No matter how rich you become, how famous or powerful, when you die the size of your funeral will still pretty much depend on the weather. —*Michael Pritchard*

The tombstone is about the only thing that can stand upright and lie on its face at the same time. —*Mary Wilson Little*

Epitaph—An irritating reminder that someone else always has the last word.
—*Gordon Bowker*

The chief problem about death . . . is the fear that there may be no afterlife, a depressing thought, particularly for those who have bothered to shave . . . I do not believe in an afterlife, although I am bringing a change of underwear.
—*Woody Allen*

LAST WORDS

What do you mean, "Keep down"? Those Rebels couldn't hit an elephant at this dist...
—*Union Maj. Gen. John Sedgewick*
(At the Battle of Spotsylvania Courthouse)

My work is done; why wait?
—*George Eastman*
(In his suicide note)

Go away. I'm all right.
—*H.G. Wells*
(1885–1946)

I've never felt better.
—*Douglas Fairbanks*

This is a very fickle and faithless generation.
—*Captain William Kidd*
(On the gallows)

You are always wanting me to give up something. What do you want me to give up this time?

I believe we must adjourn this meeting to some other place.
—*Adam Smith*

I feel better.
—*Brigham Young*

Are you sure it's safe?
—*William Palmer*
(Condemned murderer, upon mounting the gallows)

So might I safely swallow this morsel of bread, as I am guiltless of the deed.
—*Earl of Godwin*
(When accused of his brother's murder;
he choked to death on the bread.)

I am about to—or I am going to—die; either expression is used.
—*Dominique Bouhours*
(grammarian)

Dying is easy, comedy is hard.
                                              —*Edmund Gwynn*
                                              (On his deathbed)

Don't let it end like this. Tell them I said something. —*Pancho Villa*
                                              (1877?–1923)

SEX

He, in a few minutes, ravished this fair creature, or at least would
have ravished her if she had not, by a timely compliance, prevented
him.   —*Henry Fielding*

My mother told my father to tell me about the birds and the bees. He
took me to Coney Island, pointed to a couple making love under the
boardwalk and said, "Your mother wants you to know that the birds
and the bees do the same thing."   —*George Burns*

Brevity is the soul of lingerie.   —*Dorothy Parker*

Birds and bees have as much to do with the facts of life as black
nightgowns do with keeping warm.   —*Hester Mundis*

It was a blonde. A blonde to make a bishop kick a hole in a stained
glass window.   —*Raymond Chandler*
                                             Farewell, My Lovely

He gave her a look you could have poured on a waffle.
                                             —*Ring Lardner*

Anybody who believes that the way to a man's heart is through his
stomach flunked geography.   —*Robert Byrne*

It's hard to be funny when you have to be clean.   —*Mae West*

I got kicked out of ballet class because I pulled a groin muscle. It
wasn't mine.   —*Rita Rudner*

Whoever named it necking was a poor judge of anatomy.
                                             —*Groucho Marx*

A kiss that speaks volumes is seldom a first edition. —*Clare Whitting*

31

I once made love for an hour and fifteen minutes, but it was the night the clocks are set ahead.   —*Garry Shandling*

He who hesitates is a damned fool.   —*Mae West*

The mirror over my bed reads, "Objects appear larger than they are."
                                                           —*Garry Shandling*

I used to be Snow White, but I drifted.   —*Mae West*

I have an intense desire to return to the womb. Anybody's.
                                                           —*Woody Allen*

I would rather go to bed with Lillian Russell stark naked than Ulysses S. Grant in full military regalia.   —*Mark Twain*

The orgasm has replaced the Cross as the focus of longing and the image of fulfillment.   —*Malcolm Muggeridge*

I've been in more laps than a napkin.   —*Mae West*

For flavor, instant sex will never supersede the stuff you have to peel and cook.   —*Quentin Crisp*

Give a man a free hand and he'll run it all over you.   —*Mae West*

I wasn't kissing her. I was whispering in her mouth.   —*Chico Marx*
                                                           (1891–1961)

What do hookers do on their nights off, type?   —*Elayne Boosler*

Love is the only game that is not called on account of darkness.
                                                           —*M. Hirschfield*

Love is not the dying moan of a distant violin—it's the triumphant twang of a bedspring.   —*S.J. Perelman*
                                                           (1904–1979)

My brain is my second favorite organ.   —*Woody Allen*

Outside every thin woman is a fat man trying to get in.
                                                           —*Katherine Whitehorn*

It is more fun contemplating somebody else's navel than your own.
                                                           —*Arthur Hoppe*

It is better to copulate than never.   —*Robert Heinlein*

Enjoy yourself. If you can't enjoy yourself, enjoy somebody else.
                                                           —*Jack Schaefer*

Is sex better than drugs? That depends on the pusher.

—*Anonymous*

Erogenous zones are either everywhere or nowhere.

—*Joseph Heller*

I don't mind sleeping on an empty stomach provided it isn't my own.

—*Philip J. Simborg*

One figure can sometimes add up to a lot. —*Mae West*

Sex is a powerful aphrodisiac. —*Keith Waterhouse*

If I had my life to live again, I'd make the same mistakes, only sooner.

—*Tallulah Bankhead*
(1903-1968)

If all the girls who attended the Yale prom were laid end to end, I wouldn't be a bit surprised. —*Dorothy Parker*

Lead me not into temptation; I can find the way myself.

—*Rita Mae Brown*

When I'm good I'm very, very good, but when I'm bad I'm better.

—*Mae West*

Serendipity is looking in a haystack for a needle and discovering the Farmer's Daughter. —*Julius H. Comroe*

Girls are like pianos. When they're not upright, they're grand.

—*Benny Hill*

For birth control I rely on my personality —*Milt Abel*

Before sleeping together today, people should boil themselves.

—*Richard Lewis*

We practice safe sex. We gave up the chandelier a long time ago.

—*Kathy Lee Gifford*

Philip Roth is a good writer, but I wouldn't want to shake hands with him. —*Jacqueline Susann*
(1921–1974)

I was a virgin 'til I was twenty, and then again 'til I was twenty-three.

—*Carrie Snow*

Losing my virginity was a career move. —*Madonna*

For the preservation of chastity, an empty and rumbling stomach and fevered lungs are indispensable. —*St. Jerome*
(340?–420)

Chaste makes waste. —*Anonymous*

Of all the sexual aberrations, perhaps the most peculiar is chastity. —*Remy de Gourmont*
(1858–1915)

We may eventually come to realize that chastity is no more a virtue than malnutrition. —*Alex Comfort*

Celibate—A member of a union opposed to the union of members. —*Gordon Bowker*

Celibacy is not hereditary. —*Guy Goden*

Familiarity breeds contempt, but you can't breed without familiarity. —*Maxim Kavolik*

Familiarity breeds children. —*Mark Twain*

Familiarity breeds attempt. —*Goodman Ace*
(1899–1982)

We have long passed the Victorian era, when asterisks were followed after a certain interval by a baby. —*W. Somerset Maugham*
(1874–1965)

If God wanted sex to be fun, He wouldn't have included children as a punishment. —*Ed Bluestone*

I almost got a girl pregnant in high school. It's costing me a fortune to keep the rabbit on a life-support system. —*Will Shriner*

On "You Bet Your Life" a contestant told Groucho Marx that he was the father of ten children. "Why so many children?" Groucho asked. "Well, I love my wife," the contestant replied. Groucho looked at him and said, "I love my cigar, but I take it out of my mouth once in a while."

It is now quite lawful for a Catholic woman to avoid pregnancy by a resort to mathematics, though she is still forbidden to resort to physics or chemistry. —*H.L. Mencken*
(1880–1956)

Vasectomy means never having to say you're sorry. —*Anonymous*

Last night I discovered a new form of oral contraceptive. I asked a girl to go to bed with me and she said no. —*Woody Allen*

> A princess who lived near a bog
> Met a prince in the form of a frog
> Now she and her prince
> Are the parents of quints
> Four boys and one fine polliwog.
>
> —*Ogden Nash*
> *(1902-1971)*

It can be great fun to have an affair with a bitch. —*Louis Auchincloss*

She's the kind of girl who climbed the ladder of success wrong by wrong. —*Mae West*

Even in civilized mankind faint traces of monogamous instinct can be perceived. —*Bertrand Russell*
(1872–1970)

My wife has cut our lovemaking down to once a month, but I know two guys she's cut out entirely. —*Rodney Dangerfield*

It is a gentleman's first duty to remember in the morning who it was he took to bed with him. —*Dorothy Sayers*
(1893–1957)

There is a new book out that says John F. Kennedy, Jr., had an affair with Madonna. Here he is, a member of one of the America's richest and most influential families, and he's willing to stand in line just like everyone else. —*Jay Leno*

A man can sleep around, no questions asked, but if a woman makes nineteen or twenty mistakes, she's a tramp. —*Joan Rivers*

A lover without indiscretion is no lover at all. —*Thomas Hardy*
(1840–1928)

It's easy to make a friend. What's hard is to make a stranger. —*Anonymous*

Eighty percent of married men cheat in America. The rest cheat in Europe. —*Jackie Mason*

A man can have two, maybe three love affairs while he's married. After that it's cheating. —*Yves Montand*

I told my girl friend that unless she expressed her feelings and told me what she liked I wouldn't be able to please her, so she said, "Get off me." —*Garry Shandling*

My wife was in labor with our first child for thirty-one hours and I was faithful to her the whole time. —*Jonathan Katz*

Orgy—A coming together of like-minded people. —*Gordon Bowker*

Last time I tried to make love to my wife nothing was happening, so I said to her, "What's the matter, you can't think of anybody either?" —*Rodney Dangerfield*

When turkeys mate they think of swans. —*Johnny Carson*

Ever since the young men have owned motorcycles, incest has been dying out. —*Max Frisch*

I'm too shy to express my sexual needs except over the phone to people I don't know. —*Garry Shandling*

Bisexuality immediately doubles your chances for a date on Saturday night. —*Woody Allen*

If God had meant us to have group sex, he'd have given us more organs. —*Malcolm Bradbury*

It's been so long since I made love I can't even remember who gets tied up. —*Joan Rivers*

He's such a hick he doesn't even have a trapeze in his bedroom. —*Anonymous*

There is hardly anyone whose sexual life, if it were broadcast, would not fill the world at large with surprise and horror. —*W. Somerset Maugham (1874-1965)*

She was so wild that when she made French toast she got her tongue caught in the toaster. —*Rodney Dangerfield*

The difference between pornography and erotica is lighting. —*Gloria Leonard*

Get in good physical condition before submitting to bondage. You should be fit to be tied. —*Robert Byrne*

My schoolmates would make love to anything that moved, but I never saw any reason to limit myself. —*Emo Phillips*

During sex I fantasize that I'm someone else. —*Richard Lewis*

Kinky sex involves the use of duck feathers. Perverted sex involves the whole duck. —*Lewis Grizzard*

My only aversion to vice, is the price. —*Victor Buono*

There is a capacity of virtue in us, and there is a capacity of vice to make your blood creep. —*Ralph Waldo Emerson*

Man is the only animal that blushes . . . or needs to. —*Mark Twain*

Is sex dirty? Only if it's done right. —*Woody Allen*

With those delicate features of his he would have made a pretty woman, and he probably never has. —*Josefa Heifetz*

Eros spelled backwards gives you an idea of how it affects beginners. —*Anonymous*

Human beings are not animals, and I do not want to see sex and sexual differences treated as casually and amorally as dogs and other beasts treat them. I believe this could happen under the E.R.A. —*Ronald Reagan*

Oysters are supposed to enhance your sexual performance, but they don't work for me. Maybe I put them on too soon. —*Garry Shandling*

Once, while we were making love, a curious optical illusion occurred, and it almost looked as though she were moving. —*Woody Allen*

In sex as in banking there is a penalty for early withdrawal. —*Cynthia Nelms*

Sex after ninety is like trying to shoot pool with a rope. Even putting my cigar in its holder is a thrill. —*George Burns*

My wife has a one-track mind. All she thinks about is anything but sex. —*Mort Walker*

I can remember when the air was clean and sex was dirty. —*George Burns*

I hope that one or two immortal lyrics will come out of all this tumbling around.   —*Poet Louise Bogan*
(On her affair with Theodore Roethke)

Sex drive—A physical craving that begins in adolescence and ends at marriage.   —*Robert Byrne*

If it weren't for pickpockets I'd have no sex life at all.
—*Rodney Dangerfield*

I've tried several varieties of sex. The conventional position makes me claustrophobic and the others give me a stiff neck or lockjaw.
—*Tallulah Bankhead*
(1903–1968)

All this fuss about sleeping together. For physical pleasure I'd sooner go to my dentist any day.   —*Evelyn Waugh*
(1903–1966)

Nothing is so much to be shunned as sex relations.   —*St. Augustine*
(354–430)

Sex is the biggest nothing of all time.   —*Andy Warhol*

My wife gives good headache.   —*Rodney Dangerfield*

I sold my memoirs of my love life to Parker Brothers and they are going to make a game out of it.   —*Woody Allen*

The most romantic thing any woman ever said to me in bed was, "Are you sure you're not a cop?"   —*Larry Brown*

It takes a woman twenty years to make a man of her son, and another woman twenty minutes to make fool of him.   —*Helen Rowland*
(1876–1950)

After we made love, he took a piece of chalk and made an outline of my body.   —*Joan Rivers*

The reason people sweat is so they won't catch fire when making love.   —*Don Rose*

I believe in sex and death—two experiences that come once in a lifetime.   —*Woody Allen*

Sex is good, but not as good as fresh sweet corn.   —*Garrison Keillor*

A terrible thing happened again last night; nothing.   —*Phyllis Diller*

I have so little sex appeal that my gynecologist calls me "sir."
—Joan Rivers

Oh, what lies there are in kisses. *—Heinrich Heine*

A British mother's advice to her daughter on how to survive the wedding night: "Close your eyes and think of England."
—Pierre Daninos

I finally had an orgasm and my doctor told me it was the wrong kind.
—Woody Allen

My wife and I don't have mutual orgasms. We have State Farm.
—Milton Berle

It's okay to laugh in the bedroom so long as you don't point.
—Will Durst

What do I know about sex? I'm a married man. *—Tom Clancy*

My heart is pure as the driven slush. *—Tallulah Bankhead (1903-1968)*

Sex: The pleasure is momentary, the position ridiculous, and the expense damnable. *—Earl of Chesterfield*

The more the pleasures of the body fade away, the greater to me is the pleasure and charm of conversation. *—Plato (427?-348? B.C.)*

I'm tired of all this nonsense about beauty being only skin-deep. That's deep enough. What do you want, an adorable pancreas?

—Jean Kerr

MEN & WOMEN

Woman—An animal having a rudimentary susceptibility to domestication. The species is the most widely distributed of all beasts of prey, is omnivorous and can be taught not to talk. *—Ambrose Bierce (1842–1914)*

I like a woman with a head on her shoulders. I hate necks.
—Steve Martin

A lady is one who never shows her underwear unintentionally.

—*Lillian Day*

Anyone who says he can see through women is missing a lot.

—*Groucho Marx*

When confronted with two evils, a man will always choose the prettier.

—*Anonymous*

A man who won't lie to a woman has very little consideration for her feelings.

—*Olin Miller*

I hate women because they always know where things are.

—*James Thurber*
(1894–1961)

Women who miscalculate are called "mothers."

—*Abigail Van Buren*
("Dear Abby")

From birth to age 18, a girl needs good parents, from 18 to 35 she needs good looks, from 35 to 55 she needs a good personality, and from 55 on she needs cash.

—*Sophie Tucker*
(1884?–1966)

The best cure for hypochondria is to forget about your body and get interested in somebody else's.

—*Goodman Ace*
(1899-1982)

I like young girls. Their stories are shorter.

—*Tom McGuane*

I never expected to see the day when girls would get sunburned in the places they do today.

—*Will Rogers*

Some men are so macho they'll get you pregnant just to kill a rabbit.

—*Maureen Murphy*

Man is more an ape than many of the apes.

—*Friedrich Wilhelm Nietzsche*
(1844-1900)

Being a woman is a terribly difficult trade, since it consists principally of dealing with men.

—*Joseph Conrad*
(1857–1924)

There is only one good substitute for the endearments of a sister, and that is the endearments of some other fellow's sister.

—*Josh Billings*
(1818–1885)

I knew a very interesting Italian woman last winter, but now she's married. —*Percy Bysshe Shelley*
(1792–1822)

A liberated woman is one who has sex before marriage and a job after. —*Gloria Steinem*

Men have a much better time of it than women; for one thing, they marry later; for another thing they die earlier. —*H.L. Mencken*
(1880-1956)

Whatever women do they must do twice as well as men to be thought half as good. Luckily, this is not difficult. —*Charlotte Whitton*
(1896–1975)

Don't accept rides from strange men, and remember that all men are strange. —*Robin Morgan*

There are only two kinds of men—the dead and the deadly.
—*Helen Rowland*
(1876–1950)

Men are creatures with two legs and eight hands. —*Jayne Mansfield*
(1932–1967)

I refuse to consign the whole male sex to the nursery. I insist on believing that some men are my equals. —*Brigid Brophy*

The most popular labor-saving device today is still a husband with money. —*Joey Adams*

He who looketh upon a woman loseth a fender.
—*Sign in an auto-repair shop*

Of all the wild beasts of land or sea, the wildest is woman.
—*Menander*
(342?–291? B.C.)

A woman is always buying something. —*Ovid*
(43? B.C.–A.D. 18)

A woman talks to one man, looks at a second and thinks of a third.
—*Bhartrihari*
(c.625)

Woman was God's second mistake.   —*Friedrich Wilhelm Nietzsche*
(1844-1900)

Women speak two languages, one of which is verbal.
—*Steve Rubenstein*

Women who seek to be equal with men lack ambition.
—*Timothy Leary*

Women are like elephants to me. I like to look at them but I wouldn't want to own one.   —*W.C. Fields*

Can you imagine a world without men? No crime and lots of happy fat women.   —*Nicole Hollander*

If they could put one man on the moon, why can't they put them all?
—*Anonymous*

A man always remembers his first love with special tenderness, but after that he begins to bunch them.   —*H.L. Mencken*
(1880-1956)

Only a man would take time out of his busy schedule to light a fart. There's not a man in this room who hasn't seen it, heard about it or done it himself.   —*Tim Allen*

For a single woman, preparing for company means wiping the lipstick off the milk carton.   —*Elayne Boosler*

It isn't that gentlemen really prefer blondes, it's just that we look dumber.   —*Anita Loos*
(1893–1981)

She was what we used to call a suicide blonde—dyed by her own hand.   —*Saul Bellow*

Blondes have more fun because they're easier to find in the dark.
—*Anonymous*

In Biblical times, a man could have as many wives as he could afford. Just like today.   —*Abigail Van Buren*
("Dear Abby")

Men are nicotine-soaked, beer-besmirched, whiskey-greased, red-eyed devils.
—*Carrie Nation*
(1846–1911)

Men are irrelevant.
—*Fay Weldon*

I have yet to hear a man ask for advice on how to combine marriage and a career.
—*Gloria Steinem*

It is possible that blondes also prefer gentlemen.
—*Mamie Van Doren*

The turn of the century will probably be made by a woman.
—*Anonymous*

A gentleman never strikes a lady with his hat on.
—*Fred Allen*

I've never struck a woman in my life, not even my own mother.
—*W.C. Fields*

Mahatma Gandhi was what wives wish their husbands were: thin, tan and moral.
—*Anonymous*

The only time a woman really succeeds in changing a man is when he's a baby.
—*Natalie Wood*
(1938–1981)

Girls are always running through my mind. They don't dare walk.
—*Andy Gibb*

One good thing about being a man is that men don't have to talk to each other.
—*Peter Cocotas*

Talking with a man is like trying to saddle a cow. You work like hell, but what's the point?
—*Gladys Upham*

When a woman behaves like a man, why doesn't she behave like a nice man?
—*Edith Evans*
(1888–1976)

I think that maybe if women and children were in charge we would get somewhere.
—*James Thurber*

Man is a clever animal who behaves like an imbecile.
—*Albert Schweitzer*

The main result of feminism has been the Dutch Treat.
—*Nora Ephron*

The way to fight a woman is with your hat. Grab it and run.
—John Barrymore

Men and women. Women and men. It will never work.   *—Erica Jong*

Women should remain at home, sit still, keep house and bear and bring up children.
—Martin Luther

Despite my thirty years of research into the feminine soul, I have not yet been able to answer . . . the great question that has never been answered: What does a woman want?
—Sigmund Freud

The only question left to be settled now is, are women persons?
—Susan B. Anthony

There are no women composers, never have been and possibly never will be.
—Thomas Beecham

Well, it's hard for a mere man to believe that woman doesn't have equal rights.
—Dwight D. Eisenhower

But, if God had wanted us to think with our wombs, why did He give us a brain?
—Clare Boothe Luce

When men reach their sixties and retire, they go to pieces. Women just go right on cooking.
—Gail Sheehy

Woman's virtue is man's greatest invention.   *—Cornelia Otis Skinner*

I feel very angry when I think of brilliant, or even interesting women whose minds are wasted on a home. Better have an affair. It isn't so permanent and you keep your job.
—John Kenneth Galbraith

It is very difficult to run an army if the general is in love with the sergeant.
—Margaret Mead

There are two kinds of women: those who want power in the world, and those who want power in bed.
—Jacqueline Kennedy Onassis

Whether women are better than men I cannot say—but I can say they are certainly no worse.
—Golda Meir

Once made equal to man, woman becomes his superior.   *—Socrates*

Fighting is essentially a masculine idea; a woman's weapon is her tongue.
—Hermione Gingold

God made man, and then said I can do better than that and made woman.
—Adela Rogers St. Johns

No one is born a woman.   *—Simone de Beauvoir*

Women who insist upon having the same options as men would do well to consider the option of being the strong silent type.
             —Fran Lebowitz

Macho does not prove mucho.   *—Zsa Zsa Gabor*

The average woman would rather have beauty than brains because the average man can see better than he can think. *—Anonymous*

A man is as good as he has to be, and a woman is as bad as she dares.   *—Elbert Hubbard*

A woman is only a woman, but a good cigar is a smoke.
             —Rudyard Kipling

Men like to pursue an elusive woman like a cake of wet soap—even men who hate baths.   *—Gelett Burgess*

No woman ever falls in love with a man unless she has a better opinion of him than he deserves.   *—Ed Howe*

I like men to behave like men—strong and childish.
             —Françoise Sagan

What time hath scanted men in hair, he hath given them in wit.
           —William Shakespeare

The main difference between men and women is that men are lunatics and women are idiots.   *—Rebecca West*

Man is an infant, with the toys of a child, and delusions of adulthood.
             —A. Cygni

In Genesis it says that it is not good for a man to be alone, but sometimes it's a great relief.   *—John Barrymore*

HEALTH & FOOD

Body-builder—One who is fit for nothing.   *—Gordon Bowker*

It's no longer a question of staying healthy. It's a question of finding a sickness you like.   *—Jackie Mason*

I've just learned about his illness. Let's hope it's nothing trivial.
             —Anonymous

It is more profitable for your congressman to support the tobacco industry than your life.
—*Jackie Mason*

Health nuts are going to feel stupid someday, lying in hospitals dying of nothing.
—*Redd Foxx*

The trouble with heart disease is that the first symptom is often hard to deal with: Sudden death.
—*Michael Phelps, M.D.*

One of my problems is that I internalize everything. I can't express anger; I grow a tumor, instead.
—*Woody Allen*

Pessimist—Someone who can look at the land of milk and honey and see only calories and cholesterol.
—*Quote Magazine*

Attention to health is life's greatest hindrance.
—*Plato*
(427?-348? B.C.)

Flies spread disease. Keep yours zipped.
—*Anonymous*

Good health makes the practice of virtue more difficult.
—*John Bunyan*
(1628–1688)

If you don't take care of your body, where will you live?
—*Anonymous*

How can a healthy adult be so tired at the end of a day when a bird weighing under an ounce can fly nonstop across the Gulf of Mexico?
—*Edwin Pope*

People are so busy lengthening their lives with exercise they don't have time to live them.
—*Jonathan Miller*

When one has good health it is not serious to be ill.
—*Francis Blanche*

Be careful about reading health books. You may die of a misprint.
—*Mark Twain*

Exercise is bunk. If you are healthy, you don't need it; if you are sick, you shouldn't take it.
—*Henry Ford*

How can I get sick? I've already had everything.
—*George Burns*

People who feel well are sick people neglecting themselves.
—*Jules Romains*

Sleep is conducive to beauty. Even velvet looks worn when it loses its nap.
—*Joan L. Zielin*

I've been on a diet for two weeks and all I've lost is two weeks.
—*Totie Fields*
(1931–1978)

In two decades I've lost a total of 789 pounds. I should be hanging from a charm bracelet.
—*Erma Bombeck*

I'm on a seafood diet. I see food and I eat it.
—*Anonymous*

The two biggest sellers in any bookstore are the cookbooks and the diet books. The cookbooks tell you how to prepare the food and the diet books tell you how not to eat any of it.
—*Andy Rooney*

Where do you go to get anorexia?
—*Shelley Winters*

If you want to look young and thin, hang around old fat people.
—*Jim Eason*

No diet will remove all the fat from your body because the brain is entirely fat. Without a brain you might look good, but all you could do is run for public office.
—*Covert Bailey*

The waist is a terrible thing to mind.
—*Tom Wilson*

I refuse to spend my life worrying about what I eat. There is no pleasure worth forgoing just for an extra three years in the geriatric ward.
—*John Mortimer*

If this is coffee, please bring me some tea; but if this is tea, please bring me some coffee.
—*Abraham Lincoln*

A cucumber should be well-sliced, dressed with pepper and vinegar, and then thrown out.
—*Samuel Johnson*

Poets have been mysteriously silent on the subject of cheese.
—*G.K. Chesterton*
(1874–1936)

Cogito ergo dim sum. (Therefore I think these are pork buns.)
—*Robert Byrne*

Cogito ergo spud. (I think, therefore I yam.)
—*graffito*

Anybody who doesn't think that the best hamburger place in the world is in his hometown is a sissy.
—*Calvin Trillin*

You can find your way across the country using burger joints the way a navigator uses stars.
—Charles Kuralt

When compelled to cook, I produce a meal that would make a sword swallower gag.
—Russell Baker

I don't even butter my bread. I consider that cooking.
—Katherine Cebrian

I no longer prepare food or drink with more than one ingredient.
—Cyra McFadden

The most remarkable thing about my mother is that for thirty years she served the family nothing but leftovers. The original meal has never been found.
—Calvin Trillin

Some people do wonderful things with leftovers. They throw them out.
—Anonymous

Part of the secret of a success in life is to eat what you like and let the food fight it out inside.
—Mark Twain

We didn't starve, but we didn't eat chicken unless we were sick, or the chicken was.
—Bernard Malamud
(1914–1986)

In Mexico we have a word for sushi: Bait.
—José Simon

Everything you see I owe to spaghetti.
—Sophia Loren

Statistics show that of those who contract the habit of eating, very few survive.
—Wallace Irwin
(1875–1959)

Cockroaches and socialites are the only things that can stay up all night and eat anything.
—Herb Caen

Eternity is two people and a roast turkey.
—James Dent

Avoid fruits and nuts. You are what you eat.
—Jim Davis

A vegetarian is a person who won't eat meat unless someone else pays.
—Al Clethan

Cannibals aren't vegetarians; they're humanitarians.
—Anonymous

I'm not a vegetarian because I love animals. I'm a vegetarian because I hate plants.
—A. Whitney Brown

Never order anything in a vegetarian restaurant that ordinarily would have meat in it.
—*Tom Parker*

Do not make a stingy sandwich
Pile the cold-cuts high
Customers should see salami
Coming through the rye.
—*Allan Sherman*
(1924–1973)

Ask not what you can do for your country. Ask what's for lunch.
—*Orson Welles*

Continental breakfasts are very sparse. My advice is to go right to lunch without pausing.
—*Miss Piggy*

What happens to the hole when the cheese is gone?
—*Bertolt Brecht*

I will not eat oysters. I want my food dead. Not sick, not wounded, dead.
—*Woody Allen*

Only Irish coffee provides in a single glass all four essential food groups: alcohol, caffeine, sugar and fat.
—*Alex Levine*

You are where you eat.
—*Anonymous*

Life is unfair. I lost my car keys at a ball game and never found them. I lost my sunglasses at the beach and never found them. I lost my socks in the washing machine and never found them. I lost three pounds on a diet—I found them and five more.
—*Robert Orben*

I'm on a grapefruit diet. I eat everything but grapefruit.
—*Chi Chi Rodriguez*

Inside me there's a thin person struggling to get out, but I can usually sedate him with four or five cupcakes.
—*Bob Thaves*

The only way to keep your health is to eat what you don't want, drink what you don't like, and do what you'd rather not.
—*Mark Twain*

A diet is when you watch what you eat and wish you could eat what you watch.
—*Hermione Gingold*
(1897–1987)

It's okay to be fat. So you're fat. Just be fat and shut up about it
—*Roseanne*

EMOTION

I feel a very unusual sensation—if it is not indigestion, I think it must be gratitude.
—Benjamin Disraeli

Probably nothing in the world arouses more false hopes than the first four hours of a diet.
—Dan Bennett

Young gorillas are friendly but they soon learn.
—Will Cuppy

If I'm content with a little, enough is as good as a feast.
—Isaac Bickerstaffe

Anxiety is the dizziness of freedom.
—Søren Kierkegaard

Don't be afraid to take a big step. You can't cross a chasm in two small jumps.
—David Lloyd George

Everything human is pathetic. The secret source of humor itself is not joy but sorrow.
—Mark Twain

Every age is fed on illusions, lest men should renounce life early and the human race come to an end.
—Joseph Conrad

He who wonders discovers that this in itself is wonder.
—M.C. Escher

I don't have any solution, but I certainly admire the problem.
—Ashleigh Brilliant

I prefer the errors of enthusiasm to the indifference of wisdom.
—Anatole France

Happiness is seeing your mother-in-law's picture on the back of a milk carton.
—Anonymous

Happiness is the perpetual possession of being well deceived.
—Jonathan Swift

A large income is the best recipe for happiness I ever heard of.
—Jane Austen

Happiness is an imaginary condition, formerly attributed by the living to the dead, now usually attributed by adults to children, and by children to adults.
—Thomas Szasz

A lifetime of happiness! No man alive could bear it; it would be hell on earth.
—*George Bernard Shaw*

Ask yourself whether you are happy, and you will cease to be so.
—*John Stuart Mill*

If I could drop dead right now, I'd be the happiest man alive.
—*Samuel Goldwyn*

If happiness truly consisted in physical ease and freedom from care, then the happiest individual would not be either a man or a woman; it would be, I think, an American cow.   —*William Lyon Phelps*

Contempt for happiness is usually contempt for other people's happiness, and is an elegant disguise for hatred of the human race.
—*Bertrand Russell*

My life has no purpose, no direction, no aim, no meaning, and yet I'm happy. I can't figure it out. What am I doing right?
—*Charles M. Schulz*

There is only one honest impulse at the bottom of Puritanism, and that is the impulse to punish the man with a superior capacity for happiness.   —*H.L. Mencken*
(1880-1956)

There is nothing which has yet been contrived by man by which so much happiness is produced as by a good tavern. —*Samuel Johnson*
(1709–1784)

Happiness makes up in height for what it lacks in length.
—*Robert Frost*

One of the indictments of civilizations is that happiness and intelligence are so rarely found in the same person.   —*William Feather*

The one serious conviction that a man should have is that nothing is to be taken too seriously.   —*Samuel Butler*

Happiness? That's nothing more than health and a poor memory.
—*Albert Schweitzer*

This makes me so sore it gets my dandruff up.   —*Samuel Goldwyn*

It usually takes two people to make one of them angry.
—*Laurence J. Peter*

Few things are harder to put up with than the annoyance of a good example.
—*Mark Twain*

Speak when you are angry and you will make the best speech you will ever regret.
—*Ambrose Bierce*
(1842-1914)

Speak when you're angry—and you'll make the best speech you'll ever regret.
—*Laurence J. Peter*

STUPIDITY, GENIUS, WISDOM & KNOWLEDGE

The difference between genius and stupidity is that genius has its limits.
—*Albert Einstein*

To err is human
And stupid.
—*Robert Byrne*

Any girl can be glamorous; all you have to do is stand still and look stupid.
—*Hedy Lamarr*

Stupidity, like virtue, is its own reward.
—*Bill Davidsen*

Nothing spoils a good party like a genius.
—*Elsa Maxwell*
(1883–1963)

Never mistake knowledge for wisdom. One helps you make a living and the other helps you make a life.
—*Sandra Carey*

Only the shallow know themselves.
—*Oscar Wilde*
(1854-1900)

It's not only who you know, but what you know about who you know that counts.
—*Mrs. C. Lowe*

There is much pleasure to be gained from useless knowledge.
—*Bertrand Russell*

The trouble with the dictionary is that you have to know how a word is spelled before you can look it up to see how it is spelled.
—*Will Cuppy*

Ignorance has its virtues; without it there would be mighty little conversation.
—*Laurence J. Peter*

Former President Reagan seems a bit confused by all the recent furor. He called a news conference to deny ever having slept with Nancy.
—*David Letterman*

I would like to take you seriously, but to do so would affront your intelligence. —*William F. Buckley, Jr.*

Knowledge is ruin to my young men. —*Adolf Hitler*

The brain is as strong as its weakest think. —*Eleanor Doan*

You can fool too many of the people too much of the time.
—*James Thurber*

Only dull people are brilliant at breakfast. —*Oscar Wilde*
(1854-1900)

The greatest undeveloped territory in the world lies under your hat.
—*Anonymous*

Wisdom is meaningless until your own experience has given it meaning . . . and there is wisdom in the selection of wisdom.
—*Bergen Evans*

Since we cannot know all that is to be known of anything, we ought to know a little about everything. —*Blaise Pascal*
(1623–1662)

I was a freethinker before I knew how to think.
—*George Bernard Shaw*

For every credibility gap there is a gullibility fill. —*Richard Clopton*

I have never been able to understand why it is that just because I am unintelligible nobody understands me. —*Milton Mayer*

The incompetent with nothing to do can still make a mess of it.
—*Laurence J. Peter*

Consistency requires you to be as ignorant today as you were a year ago. —*Bernard Berenson*

A fellow who is always declaring he's no fool usually has his suspicions. —*Wilson Mizner*

It is impossible to defeat an ignorant man in argument.
—*William G. McAdoo*

An intellectual is a man who takes more words than necessary to tell more than he knows. —*Dwight D. Eisenhower*

An intelligence test sometimes shows a man how smart he would have been not to have taken it. —*Laurence J. Peter*

53

The most common of all follies is to believe passionately in the palpably not true. It is the chief occupation of mankind.   *—H.L. Mencken*
(1880-1956)

When we finally see the light, we see how once again we have fallen into some foolish assumption, some oafish practice, or some witless blunder.   *—Gerald M. Weinberg*
Psychology of Computer Programming

Never try to tell everything you know. It may take too short a time.
—Norman Ford

Ours is the age that is proud of machines that think and suspicious of men who try to.   *—H. Mumford Jones*

It is a very sad thing that nowadays there is so little useless information.   *—Oscar Wilde*
(1854–1900)

Wonder rather than doubt is the root of knowledge.
—Abraham Joshua Heschel

Real knowledge is to know the extent of one's ignorance.
—Confucius

MARRIAGE/RELATIONSHIPS

Marriage—A master, a mistress and two slaves, making in all, two.
—Ambrose Bierce
(1842-1914)

Many a man owes his success to his first wife and his second wife to his success.   *—Jim Backus*

Yard sale—Recently married couple is combining households. All duplicates will be sold, except children.   *—San Jose* Mercury News

'Tis more blessed to give than receive; for example, wedding presents.   *—H.L. Mencken*
(1880-1956)

Monogamy is the Western custom of one wife and hardly any mistresses.
—*H.H. Munro*
("Saki")

Marriage is based on the theory that when a man discovers a brand of beer exactly to his taste he should at once throw up his job and go to work in the brewery.
—*George Jean Nathan*
(1882–1958)

Club Med sounds fine for me. Now, where would you suggest for my wife?
—*Bill Hoest*

If you want to lose 170 pounds right away, get rid of your husband.
—*George Burns*

Wife—A former sweetheart.
—*H.L. Mencken*
(1880-1956)

The only solid and lasting peace between a man and his wife is doubtless a separation.
—*Earl of Chesterfield*
(1694–1773)

It was so cold I almost got married.
—*Shelley Winters*

I married beneath me. All women do.
—*Nancy, Lady Astor*
(1879–1964)

I tended to place my wife under a pedestal.
—*Woody Allen*

Husbands are like fires. They go out if unattended.
—*Zsa Zsa Gabor*

When a girl marries she exchanges the attentions of many men for the inattention of one.
—*Helen Rowland*

The trouble with some women is that they get all excited about nothing—and then marry him.
—*Cher*

I believe in the institution of marriage and I intend to keep trying until I get it right.
—*Richard Pryor*

Marriage has driven more than one man to sex.
—*Peter De Vries*

It destroys one's nerves to be amiable every day to the same human being.
—*Benjamin Disraeli*

Marriage is like a bank account. You put it in, you take it out, you lose interest.
—*Professor Irwin Corey*

It's relaxing to go out with my ex-wife because she already knows I'm an idiot. 	—*Warren Thomas*

He's the kind of man a woman would have to marry to get rid of.
	—*Mae West*

Marriage is a necessary evil. 	—*Menander*
	(342?–291? B.C.)

Marriage is the only war in which you sleep with the enemy.
	—*Anonymous*

Nothing anybody tells you about marriage helps. 	—*Max Siegel*

There is so little difference between husbands you might as well keep the first. 	—*Adela Rogers St. Johns*

Marriage is really tough because you have to deal with feelings and lawyers. 	—*Richard Pryor*

Marriage could catch on again because living together is not quite living and not quite together. Premarital sex slowly evolves into pre-marital sox. 	—*Gerald Nachman*

Marriage is part of a sort of 50s revival package that's back in vogue along with neckties and naked ambition. 	—*Calvin Trillin*

I'd like to get married because I like the idea of a man being required by law to sleep with me every night. 	—*Carrie Snow*

I hated my marriage, but I always had a great place to park.
	—*Gerald Nachman*

I was married by a judge. I should have asked for a jury.
	—*George Burns*

I've married a few people I shouldn't have, but haven't we all?
	—*Mamie Van Doren*

My wife and I tried to breakfast together, but we had to stop or our marriage would have been wrecked. 	—*Winston Churchill*
	(1874-1965)

To reduce stress, avoid excitement. Spend more time with your spouse. 	—*Robert Orben*

When a man brings his wife flowers for no reason—there's a reason.
	—*Molly McGee*

Any young man who is unmarried at the age of twenty-one is a menace to the community.　　　　　　　　　　*—Brigham Young*
(1801–1877)

I have known more men destroyed by the desire to have a wife and child and to keep them in comfort than I have seen destroyed by drink and harlots.　　　　　　　　　*—William Butler Yeats*
(1865–1939)

I enjoy dating married men because they don't want anything kinky, like breakfast.　　　　　　　　　　　　　*—Joni Rodgers*

Until I got married, I was my own worst enemy.　　*—Anonymous*

The poor wish to be rich, the rich wish to be happy, the single wish to be married and the married wish to be dead.　　*—Ann Landers*

Marriage is like paying an endless visit in your worst clothes.

—J.B. Priestley
(1894–1984)

Marriage is like a besieged fortress. Everyone outside wants to get in, and everyone inside wants to get out.　　　　　　*—Quitard*

The chains of marriage are so heavy it takes two to carry them, and sometimes three.　　　　　　　　　*—Alexandre Dumas*
(1802–1870)

Instead of getting married again, I'm going to find a woman I don't like and give her a house.　　　　　　*—Lewis Grizzard*

Love is blind, and marriage is a real eye-opener.　　*—Anonymous*

All men make mistakes, but married men find out about them sooner.　　　　　　　　　　　　　　　　*—Red Skelton*

In marriage a man becomes slack and selfish and undergoes a fatty degeneration of the spirit.　　　　　*—Robert Louis Stevenson*
(1850–1894)

The only thing that holds a marriage together is the husband being big enough to step back and see where the wife is wrong.
—Archie Bunker

I've been married so long I'm on my third bottle of Tabasco sauce.
—Susan Vass

Always get married early in the morning. That way, if it doesn't work out, you haven't wasted a whole day. —*Mickey Rooney*

My wife and I were happy for twenty years. Then we met.
—*Rodney Dangerfield*

My husband said he needed more space, so I locked him outside.
—*Roseanne*

I grew up in a very large family in a very small house. I never slept alone until after I was married. —*Lewis Grizzard*

A second marriage is the triumph of hope over experience.
—*Samuel Johnson*

Anyone who marries for money earns every cent of it.—*Anonymous*

Love is an ideal thing. Marriage is a real thing. A confusion of the real with the ideal never goes unpunished. —*Johann von Goethe*
(1749-1832)

Marriage is a romance in which the hero dies in the first chapter.
—*Laurence J. Peter*

All marriages are happy. It's the living together afterward that causes all the trouble. —*Raymond Hull*

If it weren't for marriage, men and women would have to fight with total strangers. —*Anonymous*

Falling madly in love with someone is not necessarily the starting point to getting married. —*Charles, Prince of Wales*

A husband is what's left of the lover once the nerve has been extracted. —*Helen Rowland*

Marriage is the only adventure open to the cowardly. —*Voltaire*

God, for two people to be able to live together for the rest of their lives is almost unnatural. —*Jane Fonda*

Marriage—a community consisting of a master, a mistress, and two slaves—making in all two. —*Ambrose Bierce*
(1842-1914)

Marriage is a great institution, but I'm not ready for an institution yet. —*Mae West*

Niagara Falls is only the second biggest disappointment of the standard honeymoon.
—*Oscar Wilde*
(1854-1900)

A wife lasts only for the length of the marriage, but an ex-wife is there for the rest of your life.
—*Jim Samuels*

Divorce is a game played by lawyers.
—*Cary Grant*

She cried, and the judge wiped her tears with my checkbook.
—*Tommy Manville*
(1894–1967)

It wasn't exactly a divorce. I was traded.
—*Tim Conway*

You don't know anything about a woman until you meet her in court.
—*Norman Mailer*

The happiest time in any man's life is just after the first divorce.
—*John Kenneth Galbraith*

One reason people get divorced is that they run out of gift ideas.
—*Robert Byrne*

My divorce came as a complete surprise to me. That will happen when you haven't been home in eighteen years.
—*Lee Trevino*

Conrad Hilton was very generous to me in the divorce settlement. He gave me 5,000 Gideon Bibles.
—*Zsa Zsa Gabor*

Divorce—The stage of marriage at which sanity prevails.
—*Gordon Bowker*

It takes two to destroy a marriage.
—*Margaret Trudeau*

Paying alimony is like feeding hay to a dead horse.
—*Groucho Marx*

Alimony is always having to say you're sorry.
—*Phillip J. Simborg*

The easiest kind of relationship for me is with ten thousand people. The hardest is with one.
—*Joan Baez*

Absence makes the heart go yonder.
—*Robert Byrne*

In a great romance, each person basically plays a part that the other really likes.
—*Elizabeth Ashley*

I love Mickey Mouse more than any woman I've ever known.
—*Walt Disney*
(1901–1966)

I'd like to have a girl, and I'm saving my money so I can get a good one.
—*Bob Nickman*

A relationship is what happens between two people who are waiting for something better to come along.
—*Anonymous*

I have such poor vision I can date anybody.
—*Garry Shandling*

The trouble with living in sin is the shortage of closet space.
—*Missy Dizick*

If you are living with a man, you don't have to worry about whether you should sleep with him after dinner.
—*Stephanie Brush*

I am a marvelous housekeeper. Every time I leave a man I keep his house.
—*Zsa Zsa Gabor*

I require three things in a man. He must be handsome, ruthless and stupid.
—*Dorothy Parker*

A woman who takes things from a man is called a girlfriend. A man who takes things from a woman is called a gigolo.
—*Ruthie Stein*

The animals most often encountered in the singles jungle are pigs, dogs, wolves, skunks, slugs and snakes. The fox is imaginary.
—*Robert Byrne*

I go from stool to stool in singles bars hoping to get lucky, but there's never any gum under any of them.
—*Emo Phillips*

Women with pasts interest men because they hope history will repeat itself.
—*Mae West*

I turned down a date once because I was looking for someone a little closer to the top of the food chain.
—*Judy Tenuta*

Have you ever dated someone because you were too lazy to commit suicide?
—*Judy Tenuta*

There is one thing I would break up over, and that is if she caught me with another woman. I won't stand for that.
—*Steve Martin*

I'm dating a woman now who, evidently, is unaware of it.
—*Garry Shandling*

Warning signs that your lover is bored
> 1) Passionless kisses
> 2) Frequent sighing
> 3) Moved, left no forwarding address — *Matt Groening*

Dating means doing a lot of fun things you will never do again if you get married. The fun stops with marriage because you're trying to save money for when you split up your property. —*Dave Barry*

Monogamous and monotonous are synonymous. —*Thaddeus Golas*

Monogamy leaves a lot to be desired. —*Anonymous*

I'm very single. I was going with someone for a few years, but we broke up. It was one of those things . . . he wanted to get married and I didn't want him to. —*Rita Rudner*

The fickleness of the women I love is only equalled by the infernal constancy of women who love me. —*George Bernard Shaw*

A correspondence course of passion was, for her, the perfect and ideal relationship with a man. —*Aldous Huxley*

The Japanese have a word for it. It's judo—the art of conquering by yielding. The Western equivalent of judo is, "Yes, dear."
—*J.P. McEvoy*

A bachelor is a man who is right sometimes. —*Laurence J. Peter*

A bachelor's life is no life for a single man. —*Samuel Goldwyn*

Rich bachelors should be heavily taxed. It is not fair that some men should be happier than others. —*Oscar Wilde*
(1854-1900)

EGOTISM/PRIDE

The last time I saw him he was walking down Lovers' Lane holding his own hand. —*Fred Allen*
(1894–1956)

Like all self-made men he worships his creator. —*Anonymous*

A narcissist is someone better looking than you are. —*Gore Vidal*

The nice thing about egotists is that they don't talk about other people. —*Lucille S. Harper*

It is far more impressive when others discover your good qualities without your help. —*Judith Martin*
("Miss Manners")

In an age when the fashion is to be in love with yourself, confessing to be in love with somebody else is an admission of unfaithfulness to one's beloved. —*Russell Baker*

If I only had a little humility, I'd be perfect. —*Ted Turner*

An egotist is a man who thinks that, if he hadn't been born, people would have wondered why. —*Dan Post*

Glendower.—I can call the spirits from the vasty deep.
Hotspur.—Why, so can I, or so can any man;
————————But will they come when you do call for them?
—*William Shakespeare*
Henry IV, Part I

MEDIOCRITY, BOREDOM & BORES

Good behavior is the last refuge of mediocrity. —*Henry S. Haskins*

Only the mediocre are always at their best. —*Jean Giraudoux*
(1882–1944)

Only a mediocre person is always at his best.
—*W. Somerset Maugham*
(1874-1965)

I don't know the key to success, but the key to failure is trying to please everybody. —*Bill Cosby*

So little time and so little to do. —*Oscar Levant*
(1906–1972)

It is time I stepped aside for a less experienced and less able man.
—*Professor Scott Elledge*
(On his retirement)

Some people stay longer in an hour than others do in a month.
—*William Dean Howells*
(1837–1920)

Do it big or stay in bed. —*Larry Kelly*

The town was so dull that when the tide went out it refused to come
back. —*Fred Allen*

The second half of the 20th century is a complete flop.
—*Isaac Bashevis Singer*

Never mistake endurance for hospitality. —*Anonymous*

Idleness is not doing nothing. Idleness is being free to do anything.
—*Floyd Dell*

It's always dullest before the yawn. —*Bob Phillips*

Some men are born mediocre, some men achieve mediocrity, and
some men have mediocrity thrust upon them. —*Joseph Heller*

Most of the evils of life arise from man's being unable to sit still in a
room. —*Blaise Pascal*
(1623–1662)

If I had it to do all over again . . . I'd have to do it all over again.
—*Tom Wilson*
"Ziggy"

Punctuality is the virtue of the bored. —*Evelyn Waugh*

Millions long for immortality who do not know what to do with themselves on a rainy Sunday afternoon. —*Susan Ertz*

The meek shall inherit the earth . . . if you don't mind. —*graffito*

Many men die at twenty-five and aren't buried until they are seventy-
five. —*Benjamin Franklin*
(1706–1790)

I'll give you a definite maybe. —*Samuel Goldwyn*

Patience *n* : A minor form of despair, disguised as a virtue.
—Ambrose Bierce
(1842-1914)

Men seldom make passes at a girl who surpasses.
—Franklin P. Adams
(1881-1960)

One machine can do the work of fifty ordinary men. No machine can do the work of one extraordinary man.   *—Elbert Hubbard*

MEMORY, THINKING & THE MIND

How to Raise Your I.Q. by Eating Gifted Children.
—Purported book title by Lewis B. Frumkes

He is indebted to his memory for his jests and to his imagination for his facts.   *—Richard Brinsley Sheridan*
(1751–1816)

The advantage of a bad memory is that one enjoys several times the same good things for the first time.   *—Friedrich Wilhelm Nietzsche*
(1844–1900)

When a book and a head collide and there is a hollow sound, is it always from the book?   *—Georg Christoph Lichtenberg*
(1742–1799)

What a strange illusion it is to suppose that beauty is goodness.
—Leo Tolstoy

What's on your mind, if you will allow the overstatement?
—Fred Allen

I prefer rogues to imbeciles because they sometimes take a rest.
—Alexandre Dumas the Younger
(1824–1895)

Great men are not always idiots.   *—Karen Elizabeth Gordon*

Nowadays the illiterates can read and write.   *—Alberto Moravia*

Cute rots the intellect.   *—Jim Davis*

Brains are an asset, if you hide them.   *—Mae West*

The intelligent man finds almost everything ridiculous, the sensible man hardly anything.
—Johann von Goethe
(1749–1832)

The only reason some people get lost in thought is because it's unfamiliar territory.
—Paul Fix

Wit is educated insolence.
—Aristotle
(384–322 B.C.)

I was gratified to be able to answer promptly. I said, "I don't know."
—Mark Twain

When ideas fail, words come in very handy.
—Johann von Goethe
(1749–1832)

You can pretend to be serious; you can't pretend to be witty.
—Sacha Guitry

Always be smarter than the people who hire you.
—Lena Horne

Ignorance is the mother of admiration.
—George Chapman
(1599?–1634)

I was going to buy a copy of *The Power of Positive Thinking*, and then I thought, "What the hell good would that do?"
—Ronnie Shakes

A great many people think they are thinking when they are merely rearranging their prejudices.
—William James

What luck for rulers that men do not think.
—Adolf Hitler
(1889–1945)

Some luck lies in not getting what you thought you wanted but getting what you have, which once you have got it you may be smart enough to see is what you would have wanted had you known.
—Garrison Keillor

An intellectual is a person whose mind watches itself.
—Albert Camus

The average person thinks he isn't.
—Father Larry Lorenzoni

Wise men talk because they have something to say. Fools talk because they have to say something.
—Plato
(427?-348? B.C.)

Confusion is always the most honest response.   —*Marty Indik*

Pessimism is a mark of superior intellect.   —*John Kenneth Galbraith*

The absence of alternatives clears the mind marvelously.
                                        —*Henry Kissinger*

Over the past ten years, for the first time, intelligence has become
socially correct for girls.   —*Tom Wolfe*

The amount of noise which anyone can bear undisturbed stands in
inverse proportion to his mental capacity.   —*Arthur Schopenhauer*

Consistency is the last refuge of the unimaginative.   —*Oscar Wilde*
                                        (1854-1900)

Forgive me my nonsense as I also forgive the nonsense of those who
think they talk sense.   —*Robert Frost*

Ignorance of ignorance is the greatest ignorance.
                                        —*Laurence J. Peter*

Don't talk to me about a man's being able to talk sense. Everyone
can talk sense. Can he talk nonsense?   —*William Pitt the Elder*
                                        (1708–1778)

If a cluttered desk is the sign of a cluttered mind, what is the signifi-
cance of a clean desk?   —*Laurence J. Peter*

When a man knows he is to be hanged in a fortnight, it concentrates
his mind wonderfully.   —*Samuel Johnson*
                                        (1709–1784)

A fine quotation is a diamond on the finger of a man of wit, and a peb-
ble in the hand of a fool.   —*Joseph Roux*

This world is comedy to those that think, a tragedy to those that feel.
                                        —*Horace Walpole*

The brain is a wonderful organ. It starts working the moment you
get up in the morning and doesn't stop until you get into the office.
                                        —*Robert Frost*

I'm going to memorize your name and throw my head away.
                                        —*Oscar Levant*

The human mind ordinarily operates at only ten percent of its
capacity—the rest is overhead for the operating system.
                                        —*Anonymous*

66

I use not only all the brains I have, but all I can borrow.
                                                    —*Woodrow Wilson*

SANITY & MADNESS

I don't really trust a sane person.   —*Lyle Alzado*
                                                    (1949-1992)

Only exceptionally rational men can afford to be absurd.
                                                    —*Allan Goldfein*

Correct me if I'm wrong, but hasn't the fine line between sanity and
madness gotten finer?   —*George Price*

A murderer is one who is presumed to be innocent until proven
insane.   —*Anonymous*

Sometimes when you look in his eyes you get the feeling that someone else is driving.   —*David Letterman*

I've always found paranoia to be a perfectly defensible position.
                                                    —*Pat Conroy*

Even paranoids have real enemies.   —*Delmore Schwartz*

A little madness in the Spring
Is wholesome even for the King.   —*Emily Dickinson*
                                                    (1830–1886)

Most men are within a finger's breadth of being mad.   —*Diogenes*
                                                    (c.412–323 B.C.)

One of the symptoms of an approaching nervous breakdown is the
belief that one's work is terribly important.   —*Bertrand Russell*
                                                    (1872–1970)

It is a far, far better thing to have a firm anchor in nonsense than to
put out on the troubled sea of thought.   —*John Kenneth Galbraith*

HUMAN ENDEAVOR

SCIENCE, INVENTION & TECHNOLOGY

Life is extinct on other planets because their scientists were more advanced than ours.   —*Anonymous*

Great moments in science: Einstein discovers that time is actually money.   —*Gary Larson*

Art is I; science is we.   —*Claude Bernard (1813–1878)*

The scientific theory I like best is that the rings of Saturn are composed entirely of lost airline luggage.   —*Mark Russell*

A science career for women is now almost as acceptable as being cheerleader.   —*Myra Barker*

We don't know a millionth of one percent about anything.   —*Thomas Edison (1847–1931)*

When the man who knows all about the fruit fly chromosomes finds himself sitting next to an authority on *Beowulf,* there may be an uneasy silence.   —*Brand Blanshard*

Astrology is Taurus.   —*F.W. Dedering*

A two-pound turkey and a fifty-pound cranberry. That's Thanksgiving dinner at Three-Mile Island.   —*Johnny Carson*

My theory of evolution is that Darwin was adopted.   —*Steven Wright*

Physics lesson: When a body is submerged in water, the phone rings.   —*Anonymous*

Help! I'm being held prisoner by my heredity and environment.   —*Dennis Allen*

Fortunately the wheel was invented before the car, otherwise the scraping noise would have been terrible!   —*Laurence J. Peter*

The guy who invented the first wheel was an idiot. The guy who invented the other three, he was the genius.   —*Sid Caesar*

He who builds a better mousetrap these days runs into material shortages, patent-infringement suits, work stoppages, collusive bidding, discount discrimination—and taxes. *—H.E. Martz*

Invention is the mother of necessity. *—Thorstein Veblen*

Getting caught is the mother of invention. *—Robert Byrne*

Humanity is acquiring all the right technology for all the wrong reasons. *—R. Buckminster Fuller*

Technology is a way of organizing the universe so that man doesn't have to experience it. *—Max Frisch*

Somehow I can't take seriously an anti-technology diatribe written on a word processor. *—Anonymous*

The generation of random numbers is too important to be left to chance. *—Robert Coveyou*
Oak Ridge National Laboratory

Things are moving too fast when we're told we can microwave Minute rice. *—Robert Orben*

The days of the digital watch are numbered. *—Tom Stoppard*

It would be as useless to perceive how things "actually look" as it would be to watch the random dots on untuned television screens.
—Marvin Minsky

It's not the things we don't know that get us into trouble; it's the things we do know that ain't so. *—Will Rogers*

Make things as simple as possible, but no simpler. *—Albert Einstein*

The significant problems we have cannot be solved at the same level of thinking with which we created them. *—Albert Einstein*

What we call progress is the exchange of one nuisance for another nuisance. *—Havelock Ellis*

Natives who beat drums to drive off evil spirits are objects of scorn to smart Americans who blow horns to break up traffic jams.
—Mary Ellen Kelly

For people who like peace and quiet: A phoneless cord.
—Anonymous

Now there's an updated version of the three R's: readin', 'ritin'—and replacin' the batteries in the calculator.   —*Nello Piccinini*

Horsepower was a wonderful thing when only horses had it.
                —*Anonymous*

ART

Art is about making something out of nothing and selling it.
                —*Frank Zappa*

Art, like morality, consists of drawing the line somewhere.
                —*G.K. Chesterton*

Art is the lie that makes us realize the truth.   —*Pablo Picasso*

Anybody who has listened to certain kinds of music, or read certain kinds of poetry, or heard certain kinds of performances on the concertina, will admit that even suicide has its brighter aspects.
                —*Stephen Leacock*

PAINTING

Once Degas witnessed one of his paintings sold at auction for $100,000. Asked how he felt, he said, "I feel as a horse must feel when the beautiful cup is given to the jockey."

This is either a forgery or a damn clever original!   —*Frank Sullivan*

The murals in restaurants are on a par with the food in museums.
                —*Peter De Vries*

I'm glad the old masters are all dead, and I only wish they had died sooner.   —*Mark Twain*

Give me a museum and I'll fill it.   —*Pablo Picasso*

Abstract Art—A product of the untalented, sold by the unprincipled to the utterly bewildered.   —*Al Capp*

Buy Old Masters. They fetch a much better price than old mistresses.   —*Lord Beaverbrook*

A painting in a museum hears more ridiculous opinions than anything else in the world.   —*Edmond de Goncourt*
                (1822–1896)

70

Bad artists always admire each other's work. —*Oscar Wilde*
(1854–1900)

In a painting I want to say something comforting.
—*Vincent van Gogh*

A subject that is beautiful in itself gives no suggestion to the artist. It lacks imperfection. —*Oscar Wilde*
(1854–1900)

A primitive artist is an amateur whose work sells. —*Grandma Moses*

For the most part theories serve only to mask the shortcomings of the artist. Theories are worked out afterwards. —*Auguste Renoir*

It is only an auctioneer who can equally and impartially admire all schools of Art. —*Oscar Wilde*
(1854–1900)

LITERATURE

It is a good thing for an uneducated man to read books of quotations.
—*Winston Churchill*
(1874–1965)

I hate quotations. —*Ralph Waldo Emerson*

A short saying oft contains much wisdom. —*Sophocles*

The majority of those who put together collections of verses or epigrams resemble those who eat cherries or oysters; they begin by choosing the best and end by eating everything.
—*Sébastien Chamfort*
(1741–1794)

What is an epigram? A dwarfish whole, its body brevity, and wit its soul. —*Samuel Taylor Coleridge*

We used to hiss the villain; now we go out and buy his book.
—*Bill Copeland*

The multitude of books is a great evil. There is no limit to this fever for writing. —*Martin Luther*
(1483–1546)

Nothing stinks like a pile of unpublished writing. —*Sylvia Plath*
(1932–1963)

Nine-tenths of all existing books are nonsense. *—Benjamin Disraeli*

Books for general reading always smell bad; the odor of common people hangs about them. *—Friedrich Wilhelm Nietzsche*
(1844-1900)

I hate books, for they only teach people to talk about what they don't understand. *—Jean-Jacques Rousseau*
(1712–1778)

Books should be tried by a judge and jury as though they were crimes. *—Samuel Butler*

Has the net effect of the invention of printing been good or bad? I haven't the slightest idea and neither has anyone else. As well ask whether it was a good or a bad plan to give over so much of the world's space to oceans. *—H.L. Mencken*
(1880-1956)

Income tax returns are the most imaginative fiction being written today. *—Herman Wouk*

Any ordinary man can surround himself with two thousand books and thenceforward have at least one place in the world in which it is possible to be happy. *—Augustine Birrell*
(1850–1933)

Studying literature at Harvard is like learning about women at the Mayo Clinic. *—Roy Blount, Jr.*

In every fat book there is a thin book trying to get out.
—Anonymous

I've given up reading books. I find it takes my mind off myself.
—Oscar Levant

Where do I find the time for not reading so many books?
—Karl Kraus
(1874–1936)

The reason why so few good books are written is that so few people who can write know anything. *—Walter Bagehot*
(1826–1877)

There are two kinds of books: those that no one reads and those that no one ought to read. *—H.L. Mencken*
(1880-1956)

Everywhere I go I'm asked if I think the university stifles writers. My opinion is that they don't stifle enough of them. There's many a best-seller that could have been prevented by a good teacher.

—*Flannery O'Connor*
(1925–1964)

The best part of the fiction in many novels is the notice that the characters are purely imaginary. —*Franklin P. Adams*
(1881–1960)

In six pages I can't even say "hello." —*James Michener*

Copy from one, it's plagiarism; copy from two, it's research.

—*Wilson Mizner*

Originality is the art of concealing your sources. —*Anonymous*

There are three rules for writing a novel. Unfortunately, no one knows what they are. —*W. Somerset Maugham*
(1874-1965)

Changing literary agents is like changing deck chairs on the *Titanic*.

—*Anonymous*

Nobody ever committed suicide while reading a good book, but many have while trying to write one. —*Robert Byrne*

It's not a bad idea to get in the habit of writing down one's thoughts. It saves one having to bother anyone else with them.

—*Isabel Colegate*

A falsehood once received from a famed writer becomes traditional to posterity. —*John Dryden*

People say that life is the thing, but I prefer reading.

—*Logan Pearsall Smith*

Some books are to be tasted, others to be swallowed, and some few to be chewed and digested. —*Roger Bacon*

Reading made Don Quixote a gentleman, but believing what he read made him mad. —*George Bernard Shaw*

Literature and vocabulary don't go together, otherwise a dictionary would be the greatest literary masterpiece. —*Laurence J. Peter*

According to his cousin, Dennis Hanks, Abraham Lincoln made books tell him more than they told other people. —*Laurence J. Peter*

In literature as in love, we are astonished at what is chosen by others.
—André Maurois

My education was the liberty I had to read indiscriminately and all the time, with my eyes hanging out. *—Dylan Thomas*

Never lend books, for no one ever returns them; the only books I have in my library are books that other folk have lent me.
—Anatole France

In the march up to the heights of fame there comes a spot close to the summit in which man reads nothing but detective stories.
—Heywood Broun
(1888-1939)

Reading is to the mind what exercise is to the body.
—Sir Richard Steele
(1672–1729)

I took a speed-reading course and read *War and Peace* in twenty minutes. It involves Russia. *—Woody Allen*

A book may be compared to the life of your neighbor. If it be good, it cannot last too long; if bad, you cannot get rid of it too early.
—H. Brooke

Books are good enough in their own way, but they are a mighty bloodless substitute for life. *—Robert Louis Stevenson*

Just the omission of Jane Austen's books alone would make a fairly good library out of a library that hadn't a book in it. *—Mark Twain*

The trouble with the publishing business is that too many people who have half a mind to write a book do so. *—William Targ*

Biography lends to death a new terror. *—Oscar Wilde*
(1854-1900)

Autobiography is a preemptive strike against biographers.
—Barbara Grizzuti Harrison

Autobiography is an unrivaled vehicle for telling the truth about other people. *—Philip Guedalla*
(1889–1944)

Autobiography is now as common as adultery and hardly less reprehensible. *—Lord Altrincham*

Autobiography is the last refuse of scoundrels.   —*Henry Gray*

A classic is a book that has never finished saying what it has to say.
                                                       —*Italo Calvino*

A man with his belly full of classics is an enemy of the human race.
                                                       —*Henry Miller*
                                                       (1891–1980)

A classic is something that everybody wants to have read and
nobody has read.   —*Mark Twain*

I do not take a single newspaper, nor read one a month, and I feel
myself infinitely the happier for it.   —*Thomas Jefferson*

The man who reads nothing at all is better educated than the man
who reads nothing but newspapers.   —*Thomas Jefferson*

There is so much to be said in favor of modern journalism. By giving
us the opinions of the uneducated it keeps us in touch with ignorance
of the community.   —*Oscar Wilde*
                                                       (1854-1900)

I always turn to the sports pages first, which record people's accomplishments. The front page has nothing but man's failures.
                                            —*Chief Justice Earl Warren*
                                                       (1891–1974)

The difference between literature and journalism is that journalism
is unreadable and literature is not read.   —*Oscar Wilde*
                                                       (1854-1900)

Never argue with people who buy ink by the gallon.
                                                       —*Tommy Lasorda*

A map marking the path of Hurricane Elena in yesterday's *News*
erroneously placed the state of Oklahoma where Missouri should
have been. The hurricane is blowing, but not that hard.
                                            —*Correction in Detroit* News

A First-Class Newspaper With Second-Class Postage Published
Weekly to Keep the Editor Out of Saloons.
                                            —*Masthead of St. Louis* Bugle

The local chapter of Parents Without Partners will sponsor an open
toga party on Saturday.   —*Napa, California* Register

Tornado watchers are on the lookout for parts of Iowa, Nebraska and Minnesota.　　　　　　　　　　　—*KPNX-TV, Phoenix, Arizona*

MUSIC

Only sick music makes money today.　—*Friedrich Wilhelm Nietzsche*
(1844–1900)

Without music, life would be a mistake.
—*Friedrich Wilhelm Nietzsche*
(1844-1900)

If Beethoven had been killed in a plane crash at the age of twenty-two, it would have changed the history of music . . . and aviation.
—*Tom Stoppard*

We aren't worried about posterity. We want it to sound good right now.　　　　　　　　　　　　　　—*Duke Ellington*
(1899–1974)

Of all the noises, I think music is the least disagreeable.
—*Samuel Johnson*
(1709–1784)

Too many pieces of music finish too long after the end.
—*Igor Stravinsky*
(1882–1971)

Bach in an hour. Offenbach sooner.　　—*Sign on a music store's door*

You want something by Bach? Which one, Johann Sebastian or Offen?　　　　　　　　　　　　　　　　—*Victor Borge*

Classical music is the kind we keep thinking will turn into a tune.
—*Kin Hubbard*
(1868–1930)

Opera in English is, in the main, just about as sensible as baseball in Italian.　　　　　　　　　　　　　　—*H.L. Mencken*
(1880-1956)

I don't know anything about music. In my line you don't have to.
—*Elvis Presley*
(1935–1977)

A gentleman is a man who can play the accordion, but doesn't.
—*Anonymous*

76

Classical music is music written by famous dead foreigners.
—*Arlene Heath*

The main thing the public demands of a composer is that he be dead.
—*Arthur Honegger*
(1892–1955)

I only know two pieces; one is "Clair de Lune" and the other one isn't.
—*Victor Borge*

When I was young we didn't have MTV; we had to take drugs and go to concerts.
—*Steven Pearl*

Music is essentially useless, as life is.
—*George Santayana*

May you all live to be 400 years old, and may the last voice you hear be mine.
—*Frank Sinatra*

No Bon Jovi breakup; Dow soars 78.71 points.
—*Headline*
—*Johnstown, PA* Tribune-Democrat

I have often thought that if there had been a good rap group around in those days, I might have chosen a career in music instead of politics.
—*Richard M. Nixon*

She Got the Gold Mine, I Got the Shaft
—*Jerry Reed song title*

I'm So Miserable Without You
It's Almost Like Having You Here
—*Steven Bishop song title*

MOTION PICTURES

If my film makes one more person miserable, I've done my job.
—*Woody Allen*

'G' means the hero gets the girl. 'R' means the villain gets the girl. And 'X' means everybody gets the girl.
—*Michael Douglas*

How am I going to do decent pictures when all my good writers are in jail? Don't misunderstand me, they all ought to be hung.
—*Samuel Goldwyn*

I arise at seven every morning, kick the alarm clock in the groin and speed to the studio. I always get a nine o'clock call, which means I shoot promptly at three in the afternoon.
—*Groucho Marx*

In this business you either sink or swim or you don't.
—*David Smith*

I saw the sequel to the movie *Clones*, and it was the same movie!
—*Jim Samuels*

We want a story that starts with an earthquake and works its way up to a climax. —*Samuel Goldwyn*

An associate producer is the only guy in Hollywood who will associate with a producer. —*Fred Allen*

The length of a film should be directly related to the endurance of the human bladder. —*Alfred Hitchcock*
(1899–1980)

Having your book turned into a movie is like seeing your oxen turned into bouillon cubes. —*John LeCarré*

If it weren't for the Japanese and the Germans, we wouldn't have any good war movies. —*Stanley Ralph Ross*

Harry, tell me the truth. How did you love my movie?
—*Spyros Skouras*

You are going to call him "William"? What kind of a name is that? Every Tom, Dick and Harry is called William. Why don't you call him Bill? —*Samuel Goldwyn*

TELEVISION & RADIO

I wish there was a knob on the TV so you could turn up the intelligence. They have one marked brightness, but it doesn't work, does it? —*Gallagher*

I find television very educational. The minute somebody turns it on, I go to the library and read a good book. —*Groucho Marx*

The human race is faced with a cruel choice: work or daytime television. —*Anonymous*

Television is democracy at its ugliest. —*Paddy Chayevsky*
(1923–1982)

The cable TV sex channels don't expand our horizons, don't make us better people and don't come in clearly enough. —*Bill Maher*

When you watch television, you never see people watching television. We love television because it brings us a world in which television does not exist. —*Barbara Ehrenreich*

Television has proved that people will look at anything rather than each other.
—*Ann Landers*

You know that humiliated feeling you get when you sneak a quick read of the *National Enquirer* in the grocery checkout line? I now get the same feeling watching "America's Favorite Home Videos," but I can't stop.
—*Mark Patinkin*

Television is more interesting than people. If it were not, we would have people standing in the corners of our rooms.
—*Alan Corenk*

Imitation is the sincerest form of television.
—*Fred Allen*

What bothers me about television is that it tends to take our minds off our minds.
—*Robert Orben*

Television has changed the American child from an irresistible force into an immovable object.
—*Laurence J. Peter*

Getting an award from TV is like getting kissed by someone with bad breath.
—*Mason Williams*

Imagine what it would be like if TV actually were good. It would be the end of everything we know.
—*Marvin Minsky*

NBC's a little jealous of CNN correspondent Wolf Blitzer. They want to get a reporter with a macho-sounding name too, so they're changing Irving R. Levine's name to Scud Schrapnel.
—*Johnny Carson*

The ultimate censorship is the flick of the dial.
—*Tommy Smothers*

My father hated radio and could not wait for television to be invented so he could hate that too.
—*Peter De Vries*

Television: Chewing gum for the eyes.
—*Frank Lloyd Wright*

Television allows you to be entertained in your home by people you wouldn't have in your home.
—*David Frost*

The polar ice cap is melting and all you can do is look at reruns of Barney Miller?
—*Bill Hoest*
"What A Guy"

CNN is one of the participants in the war. I have a fantasy where Ted Turner is elected president but refuses because he doesn't want to give up power.
—*Arthur C. Clarke*

Do you realize if it weren't for Edison we'd be watching TV by candlelight?
—*Al Boliska*

Television news is like a lightning flash. It makes a loud noise, lights up everything around it, leaves everything else in darkness and then is suddenly gone. —*Hodding Carter*

COMMUNICATION

I wish people who have trouble communicating would just shut up!
—*Tom Lehrer*

Talk is cheap because supply exceeds demand. —*Anonymous*

No comment. —*Doug Moe*
(On being named the most quotable coach in the NBA)

If the art of conversation stood a little higher, we would have a lower birthrate. —*Stanislaw Lec*

The prime purpose of eloquence is to keep other people from talking.
—*Louis Vermeil*

Most conversations are simply monologues delivered in the presence of witnesses. —*Margaret Millar*

Cutting in on some conversations is about as easy as threading a sewing machine needle when it is operating at full speed.
—*Ray Pierce*

There are very few people who don't become more interesting when they stop talking. —*Mary Lowry*

The opposite of talking isn't listening. The opposite of talking is waiting. —*Fran Lebowitz*

COMPUTERS

Computers are useless. They can only give you answers.
—*Pablo Picasso*
(1881–1973)

Part of the inhumanity of the computer is that, once it is competently programmed and working smoothly, it is completely honest.
—*Isaac Asimov*

To err is human—and to blame it on a computer is even more so.
—*Robert Orben*

The system designer suffers because the better his system does its job, the less its users know of its existence.   —*Gerald M. Weinberg*
Psychology of Computer Programming

One types the correct incantation on a keyboard, and a display screen comes to life, showing things that never were nor could be . . . however, if one character, one pause, of the incantation is not strictly in proper form, the magic doesn't work.   —*Frederick Brooks*
The Mythical Man-Month

The excuse for missing homework used to be "the dog ate it." Now it's "the disc got erased."   —*N.Z. Becher*

If debugging is the process of removing bugs, then programming must be the process of putting them in.   —*Dykstra*

Asking for efficiency and adaptability in the same program is like asking for a beautiful and modest wife—we'll probably have to settle for one or the other.   —*Gerald M. Weinberg*
Psychology of Computer Programming

If a programmer is found to be indispensable, the best thing to do is to get rid of him as quickly as possible.   —*Gerald M. Weinberg,*
Psychology of Computer Programming

The computer is down. I hope it's something serious.
—*Stanton Delaplane*

Never let a computer know you're in a hurry.   —*Anonymous*

SPORTS

There are two sorts of losers—the good loser, and the one who can't act.   —*Laurence J. Peter*

A good sport has to lose to prove it.   —*Anonymous*

Show me a good loser and I'll show you a loser.   —*Anonymous*

Show me a good loser and I'll show you an idiot.   —*Leo Durocher*

The will to win is worthless if you don't get paid for it.
—*Reggie Jackson*

Anyone can win, unless there happens to be a second entry.
—*George Ade*
(1866–1944)

Victory goes to the player who makes the next-to-last mistake.
—*Savielly Grigorievitch Tartakower*
(1887–1956)

Any fool can make a rule.
—*Henry David Thoreau*
(1817–1862)

When I feel athletic, I go to a sports bar.
—*Paul Clisura*

"No pole-vaulting, no cross-country running and no away-games."
—*Activities Director*
State Correctional Institution at Pittsburgh

Nolan Ryan is pitching much better now that he has his curve ball straightened out.
—*Joe Garagiola*

If people don't want to come out to the ball park, nobody's going to stop them.
—*Yogi Berra*

I'm no different from anybody else with two arms, two legs and forty-two-hundred hits.
—*Pete Rose*

The highlight of my baseball career came in Philadelphia's Connie Mack Stadium when I saw a fan fall out of the upper deck. When he got up and walked away the crowd booed.
—*Bob Uecker*

If a woman has to choose between catching a fly ball and saving an infant's life, she will choose to save the infant's life without even considering if there are men on base.
—*Dave Barry*

Baseball would be a better game if more third basemen got hit in the mouth by line drives.
—*Dan Jenkins*

George Steinbrenner is the salt of the earth, and the Yankee players are open wounds.
—*Scott Osler*

I probably couldn't play for me. I wouldn't like my attitude.
—*John Thompson*

A team should be an extension of the coach's personality. My teams were arrogant and obnoxious.
—*Al McGuire*

Hurting people is my business.
—*Sugar Ray Robinson*

Fishing is a delusion entirely surrounded by liars in old clothes.
—*Don Marquis*
(1878-1937)

A team is a team is a team. Shakespeare said that many times.
—*Dan Devine*
(football coach)

San Francisco has always been my favorite booing city. I don't mean the people boo louder or longer, but there is a very special intimacy. When they boo you, you know they mean you. Music, that's what it is to me. One time in Kezar Stadium they gave me a standing boo.
—*George Halas*
(1895–1983)

Football players, like prostitutes, are in the business of ruining their bodies for the pleasure of strangers. —*Merle Kessler*

When I played pro football, I never set out to hurt anybody deliberately . . . unless it was, you know, important, like a league game or something. —*Dick Butkus*

Cal quarterback Joe Kapp used to call audibles that were just obscenities directed at the other team. I like that. —*Greg Ennis*

Baseball is what we were. Football is what we've become.
—*Mary McGrory*

On Thanksgiving Day all over America, families sit down to dinner at the same moment—halftime. —*Anonymous*

College football would be more interesting if the faculty played instead of the students. There would be a great increase in broken arms, legs and necks. —*H.L. Mencken*
(1880-1956)

Fox hunting is the unspeakable in pursuit of the inedible.
—*Oscar Wilde*
(1854-1900)

The place of the father in the modern suburban family is a very small one, particularly if he plays golf. —*Bertrand Russell*

Golf is a good walk spoiled. —*Mark Twain*

Country singer Willie Nelson bought his own golf course, and replied to the question of what par was responded "Anything I want it to be. You see that hole over there? That's a par forty-seven—and yesterday I birdied it!"

If you are caught on a golf course during a storm and are afraid of lightning, hold up a 1-iron. Not even God can hit a 1-iron.

—Lee Trevino

Golf may be played on Sunday, not being a game within the view of the law, but being a form of moral effort.   *—Stephen Leacock*

If I had my way, any man guilty of golf would be ineligible for any office of trust in the United States.   *—H.L. Mencken*
(1880-1956)

Golf is a game with the soul of a 1956 Rotarian.   *—Bill Mandel*

One of the worst things that can happen in life is to win a bet on a horse at an early age.   *—Danny McGoorty*
(1901–1970)

I bet on a horse at ten to one. It didn't come in until half-past five.

—Henny Youngman

The only reason I would take up jogging is so that I could hear heavy breathing again.   *—Erma Bombeck*

Running is an unnatural act, except from enemies and to the bathroom.   *—Anonymous*

The fascination of shooting as a sport depends almost wholly on whether you are at the right or wrong end of the gun.

—P.G. Wodehouse

Skiing combines outdoor fun with knocking down trees with your face.   *—Dave Barry*

PEOPLES, CLANS & GROUPS

INDIVIDUALS AS SEEN BY OTHERS

Plato was a bore.

—*Friedrich Wilhelm Nietzsche*
(1844-1900)

Nietzsche was stupid and abnormal.

—*Leo Tolstoy*
(1828–1910)

I'm not going to climb into the ring with Tolstoy.

—*Ernest Hemingway*
(1898–1961)

Hemingway was a jerk.

—*Harold Robbins*

Harold Robbins doesn't sound like an author, he sounds like a company brochure.

—*The New Yorker*

Adam was the only man who, when he said a good thing, knew that nobody had said it before him.

—*Mark Twain*

Alexander III of Macedonia is known as Alexander the Great because he killed more people of more different kinds than any other man of his time.

—*Will Cuppy*
(1884–1949)

Working with Julie Andrews is like getting hit over the head with a valentine.

—*Christopher Plummer*

Aristotle was famous for knowing everything. He taught that the brain exists merely to cool the blood and is not involved in the process of thinking. This is true only of certain people.

—*Will Cuppy*
(1884–1949)

The affair between Margot Asquith and Margot Asquith will live as one of the prettiest love stories in all literature.

—*Dorothy Parker*
(1893–1967)

I saw Count Basie when he was nearly 80. He was playing wonderfully. Three weeks later he was dead. That guy's my hero.

—*Bob Weir, 43,*
of The Grateful Dead

[William] Bennett, who had been Secretary of Education without solving the problems of education and Drug Czar without solving the problems of drugs, now wants to write a book on how to solve the problems of both. In America, this is what we call "expertise."

—*Roger Simon*

I have played over the music of that scoundrel Brahms. What a giftless bastard!
—*Peter Ilyich Tchaikovsky*
(1840–1893)

George Bush is Gerald Ford without the pizzazz.   —*Pat Paulsen*

I worship the very quicksand he walks on.   —*Art Buchwald*
(Referring to Jimmy Carter)

Sometimes when I look at my children I say to myself, "Lillian, you should have stayed a virgin."
—*Lillian Carter*

You could have chosen war or dishonor. You chose dishonor, and now you will have war anyway.   —*Winston Churchill*
(1874-1965)
(Speaking of Neville Chamberlain,
who appeased Hitler
to achieve "peace in our time")

It is fun being in the same decade with you.
—*Franklin Delano Roosevelt*
(In a letter to Winston Churchill)

In a museum in Havana there are two skulls of Christopher Columbus; one when he was a boy and one when he was a man.
—*Mark Twain*

Calvin Coolidge didn't say much, and when he did he didn't say much.   —*Will Rogers*

Gary Cooper and Greta Garbo may be the same person. Have you ever seen them together?   —*Ernst Lubitsch*
(1892–1947)

I like DeLorean. I like his style; dig the dude's scope. He said, "I can't make stainless-steel, gull-wing, futuristic cars in the middle of a civil rebellion in Ireland, well then, I'll be the biggest cocaine dealer in Los Angeles." Style. This man knew the world wasn't conquered by Alexander the Average, Ivan the Bland or Attila the Ho Hum.

—*Gallagher*

Diogenes was asked what wine he liked best; and he answered as I would have done when he said: "Somebody else's."
—*Michel de Montaigne*

A stitch in time would have confused Einstein.   —*Anonymous*

Mr. T.S. Eliot, in choosing to live in England rather than in St. Louis or Boston, passed judgment not only on the American scene but indeed on his own fitness to adorn it.   —*W. Brogan*

Queen Elizabeth is the whitest person in the world.   —*Bette Midler*

Jerry Ford is a nice guy, but he played too much football with his helmet off.
—*Lyndon Baines Johnson*
(1908–1973)

Clark Gable's ears make him look like a taxicab with the doors open.
—*Howard Hughes*
(1905–1976)

Gary Hart is just Jerry Brown without the fruit flies.
—*Robert Strauss*

"She runs the gamut of emotions from A to B."   —*Dorothy Parker*
(Of Katharine Hepburn)

If Hitler invaded Hell, I think I would find a good word to say about the Devil in the House of Commons.   —*Winston Churchill*
(1874-1965)
(Replying to those who criticized him
for siding with Stalin during WWII)

John Houseman: His last words to us, "The theatre needs you. I'm going off to sell Volvos."   —*Robin Williams*

Howard Hughes was able to afford the luxury of madness, like a man who not only thinks he is Napoléon Bonaparte but hires an army to prove it.   —*Ted Morgan*

I read in the newspaper that they have done a psychological study of Saddam Hussein and found he has periods of contact with reality interspersed with psychotic episodes. This is known as the Peter Paul Syndrome: Sometimes you feel like a nut, sometimes you don't.
—*Jay Leno*

No doubt Jack the Ripper excused himself on the grounds that it was human nature.   —*A.A. Milne*

Henry James writes fiction as if it were a painful duty.
—Oscar Wilde
(1854-1900)

Thomas Jefferson's slaves loved him so much they called him by a special name: Dad. *—Mark Russell*

When George Jessel took Lena Horne to a famous restaurant, the doorman asked, "Who made your reservations?" Jessel replied, "Abraham Lincoln." *—Earl Wilson*

Why don't you write books people can read? *—Nora Joyce*
(To her husband, James)

He grounds the warship he walks on. *—John Bracken*
(Referring to Capt. Barney Kelly,
who grounded the U.S.S. Enterprise
in San Francisco Bay, 1983)

John F. Kennedy to his Nobel Prize-winning guests: "I think this is the most extraordinary collection of talent, of human knowledge, that has ever been gathered together at the White House—with the possible exception of when Thomas Jefferson dined here alone."

Elsa Lanchester looks as though butter wouldn't melt in her mouth, or anywhere else. *—Maureen O'Hara*

There is absolutely nothing wrong with Oscar Levant that a miracle cannot fix. *—Alexander Woollcott*

They actually banned Madonna's video from MTV? That's like being thrown out of a Marion Barry hotel party. *—Johnny Carson*

H.L. Mencken suffers from the hallucination that he is H.L. Mencken. There is no cure for a disease of that magnitude.
—Maxwell Bodenhein
(1893–1954)

Walter Mondale has all the charisma of a speed bump. *—Will Durst*

Nietzsche is peatzsche
But Sartre is smartre. *—Anonymous*

Do you realize the responsibility I carry? I'm the only person standing between Nixon and the White House. *—John F. Kennedy*
(During the 1960 presidential campaign)

He will even tell a lie when it is not convenient to. That is the sign of the great artist, you know!
—*Gore Vidal*
(Referring to Richard M. Nixon)

We need this man of action, this man of accomplishment, this man of experience, this man of courage; we need this man of faith in America . . . who has brought us to the threshold of peace.
—*Nelson Rockefeller*
(Nominating Richard M. Nixon
to his second presidential term)

If Noah had been been truly wise
He would have swatted those two flies.
—*H. Castle*

Often it does seem a pity that Noah and his party did not miss the boat.
—*Mark Twain*

I can forgive Alfred Nobel for having invented dynamite, but only a fiend in human form could have invented the Nobel Prize.
—*George Bernard Shaw*

Marie Osmond makes Mother Teresa look like a slut.
—*Joan Rivers*

Does the name Pavlov ring a bell?
—*Anonymous*

Teamster President Jackie Presser has been given a clean bill of health by the Justice Department. He won't be indicted for anything. However, because he has not bccn indicted, he may be fired for breaking Teamster tradition.
—*Mark Russell*

Reading Proust is like bathing in someone else's bathwater.
—*Alexander Woollcott*

I would like to bring you up to date on the comedian's health sweepstakes. As it stands right now, I lead Richard Pryor in heart attacks, two to one. However, Richard still leads me one to nothing in burning yourself up.
—*George Carlin*

What Einstein was to physics, what Babe Ruth was to home runs, what Emily Post was to table manners . . . that's what Edward G. Robinson was to dying like a dirty rat.
—*Russell Baker*

My father gave me these hints on speech-making:
"Be sincere . . . be brief . . . be seated."
—*James Roosevelt*

If Roosevelt were alive today, he'd turn over in his grave.
—*Samuel Goldwyn*

When they circumcised Herbert Samuel, they threw away the wrong part.   —*David Lloyd George*
(1863–1945)

Phyllis Schlafly speaks for all American women who oppose equal rights for themselves.   —*Andy Rooney*

To Theodor Geisel (Dr. Seuss), who gave me a new way to look at the neuss.   —*Dedication of Charles Osgood book*

The remarkable thing about Shakespeare is that he really is very good, in spite of all the people who say he is very good.
—*Robert Graves*

I wish Frank Sinatra would just shut up and sing.   —*Lauren Bacall*

Steven's room was a mess. Once his lizard got out of its cage, and we found it, living, three years later. He had a parakeet he refused to keep in a cage. Every week, I would stick my head in his room, grab his dirty laundry and slam the door. If I had known better, I would have taken him to a psychiatrist—and there never would have been an "E.T."   —*Leah Spielberg*

The English had Margaret Thatcher, who looks like Julia Child on Valium.   —*Robin Williams*

George Washington, as a boy, was ignorant of the commonest accomplishments of youth. He could not even lie.   —*Mark Twain*

When they asked George Washington for his ID, he just took out a quarter.   —*Steven Wright*

An empty taxi stopped and Jack Warner got out.   —*Anonymous*

Mae West had a voice like a vibrating bed.   —*John Kobal*

INDIVIDUALS AS SEEN BY THEMSELVES

Some guy hit my fender, and I said to him, "Be fruitful and multiply," but not in those words.   —*Woody Allen*

A "Bay Area Bisexual" told me I didn't quite coincide with either of her desires.   —*Woody Allen*

I never met a man I didn't want to fight.   —*Lyle Alzado*

I felt sorry for myself because I had no hands until I met a man who had no chips.
— *Kent G. Andersson*

We are here on earth to do good to others. What the others are here for, I don't know.
— *W.H. Auden*
(1907–1973)

The less I behave like Whistler's mother the night before, the more I look like her the morning after.
— *Tallulah Bankhead*
(1903-1968)

They used to photograph Shirley Temple through gauze. They should photograph me through linoleum.
— *Tallulah Bankhead*
(1903-1968)

When Sears comes out with a riding vacuum cleaner, then I'll clean the house.
— *Roseanne*

When I came back to Dublin I was court-martialed in my absence and sentenced to death in my absence, so I said they could shoot me in my absence.
— *Brendan Behan*

I'm not an ambulance chaser. I'm usually there before the ambulance.
— *Melvin Belli*

When I am dead, I hope it may be said:
"His sins were scarlet, but his books were read."   — *Hilaire Belloc*

As for me, except for an occasional heart attack, I feel as young as I ever did.
— *Robert Benchley*
(1889–1945)

A great many people have come up to me and asked how I managed to get so much done and still look so dissipated.   — *Robert Benchley*
(1889–1945)

I can't seem to bring myself to say, "Well, I guess I'll be toddling along." It isn't that I can't toddle. It's that I can't guess I'll toddle.
— *Robert Benchley*
(1889-1945)

Drawing on my fine command of the English language, I said nothing.
— *Robert Benchley*

I don't deserve this award, but I have arthritis and I don't deserve that either.
                                                                      —*Jack Benny*
                                                                      (1894–1974)

I really didn't say everything I said.   —*Yogi Berra*

Glory is fleeting, but obscurity is forever.   —*Napoléon Bonaparte*
                                                                      (1769-1821)

I have always imagined that Paradise will be a kind of library.
                                                                      —*Jorge Luis Borges*

I'm an instant star; just add water and stir.   —*David Bowie*

Let me have my own way exactly in everything, and a sunnier and pleasanter creature does not exist.   —*Thomas Carlyle*
                                                                      (1795–1881)

The Hollywood tradition I like best is called "sucking up to the stars."
                                                                      —*Johnny Carson*

I'm thirty years old, but I read at the thirty-four-year-old level.
                                                                      —*Dana Carvey*

After I'm dead I'd rather have people ask why I have no monument than why I have one.   —*Cato the Elder*
                                                                      (234–149 B.C.)

Nobody roots for Goliath.   —*Wilt Chamberlain*

Although prepared for martyrdom, I preferred that it be postponed.
                                                                      —*Winston Churchill*
                                                                      (1874-1965)

Personally I'm always ready to learn, although I do not always like being taught.   —*Winston Churchill*
                                                                      (1874-1965)

I think the American public wants a solemn ass as president. And I think I'll go along with them.   —*Calvin Coolidge*
                                                                      (1872–1933)

Being named as one of the world's best-dressed men doesn't necessarily mean that I am a bad person.   —*Anthony R. Cucci*

There are some days when I think I'm going to die from an overdose of satisfaction.   —*Salvador Dali*

Nice guys finish last, but we get to sleep in.   —*Evan Davis*

Burt Reynolds once asked me out. I was in his room.

—*Phyllis Diller*

It's a good thing that beauty is only skin deep, or I'd be rotten to the core.

—*Phyllis Diller*

I was in a beauty contest once. I not only came in last, I was hit in the mouth by Miss Congeniality.

—*Phyllis Diller*

When I go to the beauty parlor, I always use the emergency entrance. Sometimes I just go for an estimate.

—*Phyllis Diller*

Go on! Shoot me again! I enjoy it! I love the smell of burnt feathers and gunpowder and cordite!

—*Daffy Duck*

There ain't no rules around here! We're trying to accomplish something!

—*Thomas Edison*
(1847–1931)

The question isn't at what age I want to retire, it's at what income.

—*George Foreman*

Never give a party if you will be the most interesting person there.

—*Mickey Friedman*

I had a lover's quarrel with the world.

—*Robert Frost*

Unprovided with original learning, unformed in the habits of thinking, unskilled in the arts of composition, I resolved to write a book.

—*Edward Gibbon*
(1737–1794)

Gentlemen, I want you to know that I am not always right, but I am never wrong.

—*Samuel Goldwyn*

I'm proud to say I'm a humble person.

—*Edmund J. Gross*

I may have my faults, but being wrong ain't one of them.

—*Jimmy Hoffa*
(1913–1975?)

I was probably the only revolutionary ever referred to as "cute."

—*Abbie Hoffman*

If you get to be a really big headliner, you have to be prepared for people throwing bottles at you in the night.

—*Mick Jagger*

When I hear the word "culture" I reach for my gun.   —*Hans Johst*
(c. 1939)

It isn't easy being green.   —*Kermit the Frog*

People think that I must be a very strange person. This is not correct. I have the heart of a small boy. It is in a glass jar on my desk.
—*Steven King*

The nice thing about being a celebrity is that, if you bore people, they think it's their fault.   —*Henry Kissinger*

If there is another way to skin a cat, I don't want to know about it.
—*Steve Kravitz*

I can mend the break of day, heal a broken heart and provide temporary relief to nymphomaniacs.   —*Larry Lee*

There go my people. I must find out where they are going so I can lead them.   —*Alexandre Ledru-Rollin*
(1807–1874)

Success didn't spoil me; I've always been insufferable.
—*Fran Lebowitz*

People hate me because I am a multifaceted, talented, wealthy, internationally famous genius.   —*Jerry Lewis*

I worked myself up from nothing to a state of extreme poverty.
—*Groucho Marx*

Well, Art is Art, isn't it? Still, on the other hand, water is water. And east is east and west is west and if you take cranberries and stew them like applesauce they taste much more like prunes than rhubarb does. Now you tell me what you know.   —*Groucho Marx*

I talk to myself because I like dealing with a better class of people.
—*Jackie Mason*

There is only one thing about which I am certain, and that is that there is very little about which one can be certain.
—*W. Somerset Maugham*
(1874-1965)

It was such a lovely day I thought it was a pity to get up.
—*W. Somerset Maugham*
(1874-1965)

I never lecture, not because I am shy or a bad speaker, but simply because I detest the sort of people who go to lectures and don't want to meet them.
—*H.L. Mencken*
(1880-1956)

I never know how much of what I say is true.   —*Bette Midler*

I bear no grudges. I have a mind that retains nothing.
—*Bette Midler*

I thank my lucky stars I'm not superstitious.   —*Larry L. Miller*

Anybody who works is a fool. I don't work, I merely inflict myself on the public.   —*Robert Morley*

Just because your voice reaches halfway around the world doesn't mean you are wiser than when it reached only to the end of the bar.
—*Edward R. Murrow*
(1908–1965)

I would not like to be a political leader in Russia. They never know when they're being taped.   —*Richard M. Nixon*

I would have made a good Pope.   —*Richard M. Nixon*

Illegal aliens have always been a problem in the United States. Ask any Indian.   —*Robert Orben*

I should warn you that underneath these clothes I'm wearing boxer shorts and I know how to use them.   —*Robert Orben*

I was the toast of two continents: Greenland and Australia.
—*Dorothy Parker*

You'd be surprised how much it costs to look this cheap.
—*Dolly Parton*

I write down everything I want to remember. That way, instead of spending a lot of time trying to remember what it is I wrote down, I spend the time looking for the paper I wrote it down on.
—*Beryl Pfizer*

I am referred to in that splendid language (Urdu) as "Fella belong Mrs. Queen."   —*Prince Philip*
Duke of Edinburgh

I do not seek. I find.   *—Pablo Picasso*

I have left orders to be awakened at any time in case of national emergency, even if I'm in a cabinet meeting.   *—Ronald Reagan*

Well, I would—if they realized that we—again if—if we led them back to that stalemate only because that our retaliatory power, our seconds, or strike at them after our first strike, would be so destructive that they couldn't afford it, that would hold them off.
—Ronald Reagan
(When asked if nuclear war could
be limited to tactical weapons)

You make the beds, you do the dishes and six months later you have to start all over again.   *—Joan Rivers*

I'm not a real movie star—I've still got the same wife I started out with twenty-eight years ago.   *—Will Rogers*

Only in show business could a guy with a C-minus average be considered an intellectual.   *—Mort Sahl*
(Referring to himself)

I am a kind of paranoiac in reverse. I suspect people of plotting to make me happy.   *—J.D. Salinger*

When I think over what I have said, I envy dumb people.   *—Seneca*
(4 B.C.–A.D. 65)

I dote on his very absence.   *—William Shakespeare*
(1564–1616)

Though I am not naturally honest, I am so sometimes by chance.
—William Shakespeare
(1564–1616)

I haven't read any of the autobiographies about me.   *—Liz Taylor*

I stopped believing in Santa Claus when my mother took me to see him in a department store, and he asked for my autograph.
—Shirley Temple

Fame lost its appeal for me when I went into a public restroom and an autograph seeker handed me a pen and paper under the stall door.
—Marlo Thomas

I hate to advocate drugs, alcohol, violence or insanity to anyone, but they've always worked for me. —*Hunter S. Thompson*

I always wanted to be somebody, but I should have been more specific. —*Lily Tomlin*

No matter how cynical you get, it is impossible to keep up. —*Lily Tomlin*

I kissed my first girl and smoked my first cigarette on the same day. I haven't had time for tobacco since. —*Arturo Toscanini*
(1867–1957)

I never did give anybody hell. I just told the truth and they thought it was hell. —*Harry S Truman*
(1884–1972)

I am a deeply superficial person. —*Andy Warhol*

It matters not whether you win or lose; what matters is whether I win or lose. —*Darrin Weinberg*

I can't tell you if genius is hereditary, because heaven has granted me no offspring. —*James McNeill Whistler*

I never travel without my diary. One should always have something sensational to read. —*Oscar Wilde*
(1854-1900)

Dawn! A brand new day! This could be the start of something average. —*Tom Wilson*

I have bursts of being a lady, but it doesn't last long. —*Shelley Winters*

Everything I want is either illegal, immoral or fattening. —*Alexander Woollcott*
(1887–1943)

GENERAL SHOTS

I've only met four perfect people in my life and I didn't like any of them. —*Anonymous*

"I grant you that he's not two-faced," I said, " but what's the use of that when the one face he has got is so peculiarly unpleasant?" —*C.P. Snow*

The question, "Who ought to be boss?" is like asking "Who ought to be the tenor in the quartet?" Obviously, the man who can sing tenor.
—*Henry Ford*

He had the ability to be sincere without being honest.
—*Clement Greenberg*

He was so conceited it was beneath his dignity even to talk to himself.
—*Shalom Aleichem*

There was a gap between what went on in his mind and what came out of his mouth.
—*James M. Cain*

He wore baldness like an expensive hat, as if it were out of the question for him to have hair like other men.
—*Gloria Swanson*

He looked at me as if I were a side dish he hadn't ordered.
—*Ring Lardner*

His towels are monogrammed with "His" and "Next."
—*Alan Levine*

She'd have the last word with an echo.
—*Edna McCann*

She had the Midas touch. Everything she touched turned into a muffler.
—*Lisa Smerling*

Leroy is a self-made man, which shows what happens when you don't follow directions.
—*Bill Hoest*
"The Lockhorns"

She's descended from a long line her mother listened to.
—*Gypsy Rose Lee*
(1914–1970)

I must decline your invitation owing to a subsequent engagement.
—*Oscar Wilde*
(1854-1900)

I can't believe that out of 100,000 sperm, you were the quickest.
—*Steven Pearl*

His mother should have thrown him away and kept the stork.
—*Mae West*

Every time I look at you I get a fierce desire to be lonesome.
—*Oscar Levant*

No one can have a higher opinion of him than I have, and I think he's a dirty little beast.
—*W.S. Gilbert*
(1836–1911)

When your I.Q. rises to 28, sell.
—*Professor Irwin Corey*

He had a winning smile, but everything else was a loser.
—*George C. Scott*

She had two complexions, A.M. and P.M.
—*Ring Lardner*

He writes so well he makes me feel like putting my quill back in my goose.
—*Fred Allen*
(1894–1956)

He can compress the most words into the smallest idea of any man I ever met.
—*Abraham Lincoln*

NATIONS, STATES & ETHNICITY

A nation . . . is just a society for hating foreigners.
—*Olaf Stapledon*

Naturalized Citizen—One who becomes a citizen with his clothes on.
—*Laurence J. Peter*

I went around the world last year and you want to know something? It hates each other.
—*Edward J. Mannix*

To travel is to discover that everyone is wrong about other countries.
—*Aldous Huxley*
(1894–1963)

Immigration is the sincerest form of flattery.
—*Jack Parr*

Men and nations behave wisely once they have exhausted all other alternatives.
—*Abba Eban*

A nation is a society united by a delusion about its ancestry and by common hatred of its neighbors.
—*Dean William R. Inge*

When asked by an anthropologist what the Indians called America before the white man came, an Indian said simply, "Ours."
—*Vine Deloria, Jr.*

I tremble for my country when I reflect that God is just.

—*Thomas Jefferson*
(1743–1826)

Americans are a race of convicts and ought to be thankful for anything we allow them short of hanging.　　　—*Samuel Johnson*

America is the country where you buy a lifetime supply of aspirin for one dollar, and use it up in two weeks.　　　—*John Barrymore*

The 100% American is 99% idiot.　　　—*George Bernard Shaw*

The genius of you Americans is that you never make clear-cut stupid moves, only complicated stupid moves which make us wonder at the possibility that there may be something to them we are missing.

—*Gamel Abdel Nasser*
(1918–1970)

America is a large friendly dog in a small room. Every time it wags its tail it knocks over a chair.　　　—*Arnold Toynbee*
(1889–1975)

America is a mistake, a giant mistake.　　　—*Sigmund Freud*

The United States is like the guy at the party who gives cocaine to everybody and still nobody likes him.　　　—*Jim Samuels*

Americans will put up with anything provided it doesn't block traffic.

—*Dan Rather*

Thanks to the Interstate Highway System, it is now possible to travel from coast to coast without seeing anything.　　　—*Charles Kuralt*

If all the cars in the United States were placed end to end, it would probably be Labor Day weekend.　　　—*Doug Larson*

In some parts of the world, people still pray in the streets. In this country they're called pedestrians.　　　—*Gloria Pitzer*

America is the only country that went from barbarism to decadence without civilization in between.　　　—*Oscar Wilde*
(1854-1900)

America is a fortunate country. She grows by the follies of our European nations.　　　—*Napoléon Bonaparte*
(1769-1821)

I'm very critical of the U.S., but get me outside the country and all of a sudden I can't bring myself to say one nasty thing about the U.S.
—Saul Alinsky
(1902–1972)

Rivers in the United States are so polluted that acid rain makes them cleaner. *—Andrew Malcolm*

There are no second acts in American lives. *—F. Scott Fitzgerald*
(1896–1940)

We have really everything in common with America nowadays except, of course, language. *—Oscar Wilde*
(1854-1900)

I wonder if anybody ever reached the age of thirty-five in New England without wanting to kill himself. *—Barrett Wendell*
(1855–1921)

Living in California adds ten years to a man's life. And those extra ten years I'd like to spend in New York. *—Harry Ruby*

I just got wonderful news from my real estate agent in Florida. They found land on my property. *—Milton Berle*

I moved to Florida because you don't have to shovel water.
—James Randi

It is true that I was born in Iowa, but I can't speak for my twin sister.
—Abigail Van Buren
("Dear Abby")

Nebraska is proof that Hell is full and the dead walk the earth.
—Liz Winston

You have to feel sorry for all those convicts in New Hampshire stamping out license plates that say "Live Free or Die."
—Anonymous

Most Texans think Hanukkah is some sort of duck call.
—Richard Lewis

You can always tell a Texan, but not much. *—Anonymous*

Texans are proof that the world was populated by aliens.
—Cynthia Nelms

The big cities of America are becoming Third World countries.
—*Nora Ephron*

The town where I grew up has a zip code of E-I-E-I-O.
—*Martin Mull*

I enjoyed *Gone With The Wind.* Frankly, I've never seen Atlanta looking better!
—*Maria Todd*

I have just returned from Boston. It is the only thing to do if you find yourself there.
—*Fred Allen*

In Buffalo, suicide is redundant.
—from *A Chorus Line*

It's a hundred and six miles to Chicago. We've got a full tank of gas, half a pack of cigarettes, it's dark and we're wearing sunglasses. Hit it!
—*The Blues Brothers*

That's great advertising when you can turn Chicago into a city you'd want to spend more than three hours in.
—*Jerry Della Femina*

A gourmet restaurant in Cincinnati is one where you leave the tray on the table after you eat.
—*Anonymous*

In Green Bay, Wisconsin, ten bowling shirts are considered a great wardrobe.
—*Guy Koch*

There is nothing wrong with Hollywood that six first-class funerals wouldn't solve.
—*Anonymous*

Hollywood is a place where they'll pay you a thousand dollars for a kiss and fifty cents for your soul.
—*Marilyn Monroe*

Behind the phony tinsel of Hollywood lies the real tinsel.
—*Oscar Levant*

It isn't necessary to have relatives in Kansas City in order to be unhappy.
—*Groucho Marx*

That's the news from Lake Woebegon, where all the men are smart, the women are good- looking and all the children are above average.
—*Garrison Keillor*

The difference between Los Angeles and yoghurt is that yoghurt has an active, living culture.
—*Anonymous*

Isn't it nice that people who prefer Los Angeles to San Francisco live there?
—*Herb Caen*

Tip the world over on its side and everything loose will land in Los
Angeles.   —*Frank Lloyd Wright*

Oh, to be in L.A. when the polyethyl-vinyl trees are in bloom.
                                            —*Herb Gold*

Miami Beach is where neon goes to die.   —*Lenny Bruce*

Happiness is Seeing Lubbock, Texas, in the Rearview Mirror.
                                            —*Song Title*

New York: Where everyone mutinies but no one deserts.
                                            —*Harry Hershfield*

In San Francisco, Halloween is redundant.   —*Will Durst*

Washington is a city of southern efficiency and northern charm.
                                            —*John F. Kennedy*
                                            (1917-1963)

The fantasy of every Australian man is to have two women—one
cleaning and the other dusting.   —*Maureen Murphy*

On the Beach is a film about the end of the world and I couldn't think
of a better place to film it.   —*Ava Gardner*
                                     (On Melbourne, Australia)

Over many decades the citizens of Darwin fell into two categories—
those who were paid to stay there and those who had no money to
leave.   —*Ernestine Hill*

Canada is the vichyssoise of nations; it's cold, half French and difficult to stir.   —*Stuart Keate*

It has been 45 years since we fought with the Americans in World
War II. For the first time since then, we have been able to assert our
independence, to ignore the dictates of Moscow. We are happy to be
back.   —*Lt. Colonel Lubomir Smeyhlik*
                        (Czechoslovakian Army in Saudi Arabia)

One day there will be only five kings left: hearts, spades, diamonds,
clubs and England.   —*King Farouk of Egypt*
                                            (1920–1965)

Boy, the things I do for England.   —*Charles, Prince of Wales*
                                     (On sampling snake meat)

To disagree with three-fourths of the British public is one of the first requisites of sanity.
—*Oscar Wilde*
(1854-1900)

The nation had the lion's heart. I had the luck to give the roar.
—*Winston Churchill*
(1874-1965)

If England treats her criminals the way she has treated me, she doesn't deserve to have any.
—*Oscar Wilde*
(1854–1900)

France is a country where the money falls apart and you can't tear the toilet paper.
—*Billy Wilder*

If it were not for the government, we would have nothing to laugh at in France.
—*Sébastien Chamfort*
(1740–1794)

In Paris, they simply stared when I spoke to them in French; I never did succeed in making those idiots understand their own language.
—*Mark Twain*

Iraq won the toss, and has elected to receive.
—*Sign on Hilton Hotel*
Riyadh, Saudi Arabia

In Ireland, a writer is looked upon as a failed conversationalist.
—*Anonymous*

May the enemies of Ireland never eat bread nor drink whisky, but be tormented with itching without benefit of scratching.
—*Traditional St. Patrick's Day toast*

In Italy a woman can have a face like a train wreck if she's blonde.
—*Anonymous*

Where but in Kenya can a man whose grandfather was a cannibal watch a really good game of polo?
—*Marina Sulzberger*
(1920–1976)

The Russians love Brooke Shields because her eyebrows remind them of Leonid Brezhnev.
—*Robin Williams*

If this is your first visit to the U.S.S.R., you are welcome to it.
—*Notice in Intourist hotel in Moscow*

Not that I dislike McDonald's, but things must be pretty bad in
Moscow if people are willing to wait three hours for large fries.
—Mark Patinkin

Gaiety is the most outstanding feature of the Soviet Union.
—Joseph Stalin
(1879–1953)

There is a new awareness of style in the Soviet Union. The premier's
wife recently appeared on the cover of *House and Tractor.*
—Johnny Carson

In Italy, for thirty years under the Borgias, they had warfare, terror,
murder and bloodshed, but they produced Michelangelo, Leonardo
da Vinci and the Renaissance. In Switzerland, they had brotherly
love, they had five hundred years of democracy and peace, and what
did they produce? The cuckoo clock.   *—Graham Greene*
The Third Man

The food in Yugoslavia is either very good or very bad. One day they
served us fried chains.   *—Mel Brooks*

There are still parts of Wales where the only concession to gaiety is a
striped shroud.   *—Gwyn Thomas*

PROVERBS

I do not say a proverb is amiss when aptly and reasonably applied,
but to be forever discharging them, right or wrong, hit or miss, ren-
ders conversation insipid and vulgar.   *—Miguel de Cervantes*
(1547–1616)

The most dangerous food is wedding cake.   *—American proverb*

Trust in Allah, but tie your camel.   *—Arab proverb*

Throw a lucky man in the sea, and he will come up with a fish in his
mouth.   *—Arab proverb*

Divorce is the sacrament of adultery.   *—French proverb*

White hair is not a sign of wisdom, only age.   *—Greek proverb*

Do not insult the mother alligator until after you have crossed the
river.   *—Haitian proverb*

Strife is better than loneliness. —*Irish proverb*

It is better to be a coward for a minute than dead for the rest of your life. —*Irish proverb*

The best way to get praise is to die. —*Italian proverb*

Bed is the poor man's opera. —*Italian proverb*

The nail that sticks up gets hammered down. —*Japanese proverb*

A man in love mistakes a pimple for a dimple. —*Japanese proverb*

A louse in the cabbage is better than no meat at all.
—*Pennsylvania-Dutch proverb*

His absence is good company. —*Scottish proverb*

Whoever tells the truth is chased out of nine villages.
—*Turkish proverb*

HISTORY & THE ANCIENTS

The first human being who hurled an insult instead of a stone was the founder of civilization. —*Sigmund Freud*

Civilization exists by geological consent, subject to change without notice. —*Will Durant*

Things have never been more like the way they are today in history.
—*Dwight David Eisenhower*
(1890–1969)

History will be kind to me for I intend to write it.
—*Winston Churchill*
(1874-1965)

One of the lessons of history is that nothing is often a good thing to do and always a clever thing to say. —*Will Durant*

The Romans would never have found time to conquer the world if they had been obliged first to learn Latin. —*Heinrich Heine*

The man who has nothing to boast of but his ancestry is like a potato. The only good belonging to him is underground.
—*Sir Thomas Overbury*

Posterity is as likely to be wrong as anybody else.

—Heywood Broun
(1888-1939)

History is a set of lies agreed upon.   *—Napoléon Bonaparte*
(1769-1821)

History is an account, mostly false, of events, mostly unimportant, which are brought about by rulers, mostly knaves, and soldiers, mostly fools.   *—Ambrose Bierce*
(1842-1914)

Human history becomes more and more a race between education and catastrophe.   *—H.G. Wells*

The history of ideas is the history of the grudges of solitary men.
—E.M. Cioran

The present is the period when the future pauses for a short while before becoming the past.   *—Laurence J. Peter*

Historical reminder: Always put Horace before Descartes.
—Donald O. Rickter

What a time! What a civilization!   *—Cicero*
(106–43 B.C.)

The budget should be balanced, the treasury refilled, public debt reduced, the arrogance of officialdom tempered and controlled, and the assistance to foreign lands curtailed, lest Rome become bankrupt.   *—Cicero*
(106–43 B.C.)

Oh, this age! How tasteless and ill-bred it is!   *—Catullus*
(87?–54? B.C.)

Very few things happen at the right time and the rest do not happen at all. The conscientious historian will correct these defects.
—Herodotus
(484–425 B.C.)

How little you know about the age you live in if you think that honey is sweeter than cash in hand.   *—Ovid*
(43? B.C.–A.D. 18)

VOCATIONS, AVOCATIONS & THOUGHT

GOD, THE GODS & THE UNIVERSE

The gods too are fond of a joke.

—Aristotle
(384–322 B.C.)

Man is certainly stark mad. He cannot make a worm, and yet he will be making gods by the dozen.

—Michel de Montaigne
(1533–1592)

If I had been present at creation, I would have given some useful hints.

—Alfonso the Wise
(1221–1284)

Imagine the Lord talking French! Aside from a few odd words in Hebrew, I took it completely for granted that God had never spoken anything but the most dignified English.

—Clarence Day

God doesn't have to put his name on a label in the corner of a meadow because nobody else makes meadows.

—Cecil Laird

How can I believe in God when just last week I got my tongue caught in the roller of an electric typewriter?

—Woody Allen

God help those who do not help themselves.

—Wilson Mizner

It is the final proof of God's omnipotence that he need not exist in order to save us.

—Peter De Vries

God is not dead, but alive and well and working on a much less ambitious project.

—graffito

Why attack God? He may be as miserable as we are.

—Erik Satie
(1866–1925)

The only thing that stops God from sending another flood is that the first one was useless.

—Sébastien Chamfort
(1741–1794)

God is dead, but fifty thousand social workers have risen to take his place.

—J.D. McCoughey

Which is it, is man one of God's blunders or is God one of man's?
—*Friedrich Wilhelm Nietzsche*
(1844–1900)

God seems to have left the receiver off the hook.   —*Arthur Koestler*

Chance is perhaps the pseudonym of God when He did not want to sign.   —*Anatole France*

Man is Creation's masterpiece; but who says so?   —*Elbert Hubbard*

If God had meant us to go metric, why did he give Christ twelve apostles?   —*Gyles Brandreth*

What can you say about a society that says that God is dead and Elvis is alive?   —*Irv Kupcinet*

Your chances of getting hit by lightning go up if you stand under a tree, shake your fist at the sky, and say, "Storms suck!"
—*Johnny Carson*

God made everything out of nothing, but the nothingness shows through.   —*Christopher Morley*
(1890–1957)

I'm astounded by people who want to "know" the universe when it's hard enough to find your way around Chinatown.   —*Woody Allen*

Sometimes I think the surest sign that intelligent life exists elsewhere in the universe is that none of it has tried to contact us.
—*Bill Watterson*

RELIGION, BELIEFS & SCRIPTURE

We must respect the other fellow's religion, but only in the sense and to the extent that we respect his theory that his wife is beautiful and his children smart.   —*H.L. Mencken*
(1880–1956)

Religion is what keeps the poor from murdering the rich.
—*Napoléon Bonaparte*
(1769–1821)

Religions change; beer and wine remain.   —*Hervey Allen*
(1889–1949)

Churches welcome all denominations, but most prefer tens and twenties.   —*Anonymous*

A difference of opinion is what makes horse racing and missionaries.
—*Will Rogers*

Do television evangelists do more than lay people?
—*Stanley Ralph Ross*

A pious man is one who would be an atheist if the king were.
—*Jean de La Bruyère*
(1645–1696)

I detest converts almost as much as I do missionaries.
—*H.L. Mencken*
(1880-1956)

In Burbank there's a drive-in church called Jack-in-the-Pew. You shout your sins into the face of a plastic priest.   —*Johnny Carson*

Ethical Man—A Christian holding four aces.   —*Mark Twain*

Going to church doesn't make you a Christian any more than going to the garage makes you a car.   —*Laurence J. Peter*

The trouble with born-again Christians is that they are an even bigger pain the second time around.   —*Herb Caen*

Promise me that if you become a Christian you'll become a Presbyterian.   —*Lord Beaverbrook*
(To Joseph Stalin, 1941)

There's nothing like a Catholic wedding to make you wish that life had a fast-forward button.   —*Dan Chopin*

Every day people are straying away from the church and going back to God.   —*Lenny Bruce*
(1923–1966)

Catholicism has changed tremendously in recent years. Now when Communion is served there is also a salad bar.   —*Bill Marr*

He was of the faith chiefly in the sense that the church he currently did not attend was Catholic.   —*Kingsley Amis*

The Vatican is against surrogate mothers. Good thing they didn't have that rule when Jesus was born.   —*Elayne Boosler*

The history of saints is mainly the history of insane people.
—*Benito Mussolini*
(1883–1945)

When I was a kid in the ghetto, a gang started going around harassing people, so some of the toughest kids formed a gang called the Sharks to stop them. The other gang was called the Jehovah's Witnesses. —*Charles Kosar*

My karma ran over your dogma. —*Anonymous*

Most of us spend the first six days of the week sowing wild oats, then we go to church on Sunday and pray for a crop failure. —*Fred Allen*

Martyrs set bad examples. —*David Russell*

Some things have to be believed to be seen. —*Ralph Hodgson*

There are some things only intellectuals are crazy enough to believe. —*George Orwell*

I never cease being dumfounded by the unbelievable things people believe. —*Leo Rosten*

Sometimes I've believed as many as six impossible things before breakfast. —*Lewis Carroll (Charles Lutwidge Dodgson) (1832-1898)*

Oh, what a tangled web we weave when first we practice to believe. —*Laurence J. Peter*

Generally, the theories we believe we call facts, and the facts we disbelieve we call theories. —*Felix Cohen*

We are inclined to believe those we do not know, because they have never deceived us. —*Samuel Johnson (1709–1784)*

Seeing is deceiving. It's eating that's believing. —*James Thurber*

What matters today is not the difference between those who believe and those who do not believe, but the difference between those who care and those who don't. —*Abbé Pire*

A belief is not true because it is useful. —*Henri Frédéric Amiel (1821–1881)*

There are two ways to slide easily through life; to believe everything or to doubt everything; both ways save us from thinking. —*Alfred Karzybski*

Nothing is so firmly believed as that which is least known.
—Michel de Montaigne
(1533–1592)

A man must not swallow more beliefs than he can digest.
—Brooks Adams

Every man prefers belief to the exercise of judgment.   *—Seneca*
(4 B.C.–A.D. 65)

If you don't count some of Jehovah's injunctions, there are no
humorists in the Bible.   *—Mordecai Richler*

The bible shows the way to go to heaven, not the way the heavens
go.   *—Galileo*

Scriptures, n. The sacred books of our holy religion, as distinguished
from the false and profane writings on which all other faiths are
based.   *—Ambrose Bierce*
(1842–1914)

The total absence of humor from the Bible is one of the most singu-
lar things in all literature.   *—Alfred North Whitehead*
(1861–1947)

The Good Book—one of the most remarkable euphemisms ever
coined.   *—Ashley Montagu*

So far as I can remember, there is not one word in the Gospels in
praise of intelligence.   *—Bertrand Russell*

When the white man came we had the land and they had the Bibles;
now they have the land and we have the Bibles. *—Chief Dan George*

These things are good in little measure and evil in large: yeast, salt
and hesitation.   *—The Talmud*

MORALITY, TRUTH & CONSCIENCE

Immorality: the morality of those who are having a better time.
—*H.L. Mencken*
(1880–1956)

If once a man indulges himself in murder, very soon he comes to think little of robbing, and from robbing he next comes to drinking and Sabbath-breaking, and from that to incivility and procrastination.
—*Thomas De Quincey*
(1785–1859)

Be as nice as possible and as nasty as necessary.   —*Al Neuharth*

Always be sincere, even when you don't mean it.   —*Irene Peter*

I am not sincere, not even when I say I am not.   —*Jules Renard*

A little sincerity is a dangerous thing, and a great deal of it is absolutely fatal.   —*Oscar Wilde*
(1854–1900)

It is easier to be gigantic than to be beautiful.
—*Friedrich Wilhelm Nietzsche*
(1844–1900)

Propaganda is the art of persuading others of what you don't believe yourself.   —*Abba Eban*
People today are wearing things on their T-shirts that they once wouldn't dare tell their analysts.   —*Chicago* Sun-Times

Never believe anything until it has been officially denied.
—*Claude Cockburn*
(1904–1981)

Temptations, unlike opportunities, will always give you many second chances.   —*O.A. Battista*

After his Cabinet had voted "No" on the issue of emancipation, Lincoln raised his right hand and said, "The ayes have it."
—*Laurence J. Peter*

The trouble with the rat race is that even if you win, you're still a rat.

—*Lily Tomlin*

Virtue has never been as respectable as money.   —*Mark Twain*

O Lord, help me to be pure, but not yet.

—*St. Augustine*
(354–430)

An evil mind is a constant solace.

—*Anonymous*

A thing worth having is a thing worth cheating for.

—*W.C. Fields*

He without benefit of scruples
His fun and money soon quadruples.

—*Ogden Nash*
(1902–1971)

It has been my experience that folks who have no vices have very few virtues.

—*Abraham Lincoln*

My only aversion to vice is the price.

—*Victor Buono*

It is hard to look up to a leader who keeps his ear to the ground.

—*James H. Boren*

Virtue is insufficient temptation.

—*George Bernard Shaw*

Nothing spoils a confession like repentance.

—*Anatole France*

Is not the whole world a vast house of assignation to which the filing system has been lost?

—*Quentin Crisp*

Ours would be a better country if people would just obey two of the Ten Commandments. Any two.

—*Michael Sovern*
Ex-President, Columbia University

Scandal is gossip made tedious by morality.

—*Oscar Wilde*
(1854–1900)

There are times when you have to choose between being human and having good taste.

—*Bertolt Brecht*

Most of the evils of life arise from man's being unable to sit still in a room.

—*Blaise Pascal*
(1623–1662)

He has every attribute of a dog except loyalty.

—*Senator Thomas P. Gore*

Fiction is obliged to stick to possibilities. Truth isn't.

—*Mark Twain*

A lie is an abomination unto the Lord and an ever present help in times of trouble.

—*Adlai Stevenson*
(1900–1965)

If you tell the truth you don't have to remember anything.
—*Mark Twain*

Truth is shorter than fiction.   —*Irving Cohen*

Under current law, it is a crime for a private citizen to lie to a government official, but not for the government official to lie to the people.
—*Donald M. Fraser*

As scarce as truth is, the supply has always been in excess of the demand.   —*Josh Billings*
(1818–1885)

One of the most striking differences between a cat and a lie is that a cat has only nine lives.   —*Mark Twain*

George Washington, as a boy, was ignorant of the commonest accomplishments of youth. He could not even lie.   —*Mark Twain*

There are only two ways of telling the complete truth—Anonymously and posthumously.   —*Thomas Sowell*

Truth is more of a stranger than fiction.   —*Mark Twain*

If language be not in accordance with the truth of things, affairs cannot be carried on to success.   —*Confucius*

Many people would be more truthful were it not for their uncontrollable desire to talk.   —*Edward Watson Howe*

Actions lie louder than words.   —*Carolyn Wells*

In order to preserve your self–respect, it is sometimes necessary to lie and cheat.   —*Robert Byrne*

It is always the best policy to tell the truth, unless, of course, you are an exceptionally good liar.   —*Jerome K. Jerome*

A lie can travel halfway around the world while the truth is putting on its shoes.   —*Mark Twain*

Man will occasionally stumble over the truth, but most of the time he will pick himself up and continue on.   —*Winston Churchill*
(1874–1965)

Living with a conscience is like driving a car with the brakes on.

—*Budd Schulberg*

A clear conscience is often the sign of a bad memory.   —*Anonymous*

Conscience is a mother-in-law whose visit never ends.

—*H.L. Mencken*
(1880–1956)

Philanthropist *n* : A rich (and usually bald) old gentleman who has trained himself to grin while his conscience is picking his pocket.

—*Ambrose Bierce*
(1842–1914)

ALCOHOL & OTHER DRUGS

If alcohol is a crutch, then Jack Daniel's is the wheelchair. Eight glasses and you forget the English language. You just have one massive vowel movement. —*Robin Williams*

Water, taken in moderation, cannot hurt anybody. —*Mark Twain*

The best audience is intelligent, well-educated and a little drunk.

—*Alben W. Barkley*
(1877–1956)

Drunk—A miracle worker who, while being unable to walk on water, is frequently to be seen staggering on whiskey. —*Gordon Bowker*

Reminds me of my safari in Africa. Somebody forgot the corkscrew and for several days we had to live on nothing but food and water.

—*W.C. Fields*

Sometimes too much to drink is barely enough. —*Mark Twain*

Like a camel, I can go without a drink for seven days—and have on several horrible occasions. —*Herb Caen*

Winston Churchill's habit of guzzling a quart or two a day of good cognac is what saved civilization from the Luftwaffe, Hegelian logic, Wagnerian love-deaths and potato pancakes. —*Charles McCabe*
(1915–1983)

I've never been drunk, but often I've been overserved.

—*George Gobel*

I feel sorry for people who don't drink, because when they get up in the morning, they're not going to feel any better all day.

—*Phil Harris*

Hangover—The mourning after the night before. —*Gordon Bowker*

Once, during Prohibition, I was forced to live for days on nothing but food and water.
—*W.C. Fields*

I drink too much. Last time I gave a urine sample there was an olive in it.
—*Rodney Dangerfield*

Work is the curse of the drinking classes.
—*Oscar Wilde*
(1854–1900)

I drink no more than a sponge.
—*Rabelais*
(1494–1553)

A drinker has a hole under his nose that all his money runs into.
—*Thomas Fuller*
(1608–1661)

'Twas a woman who drove me to drink, and I never had the courtesy to thank her for it.
—*W.C. Fields*
(1880–1946)

One more drink and I'll be under the host.
—*Dorothy Parker*

Inflation has gone up over a dollar a quart.
—*W.C. Fields*
(1880–1946)

Even though a number of people have tried, no one has yet found a way to drink for a living.
—*Jean Kerr*

I haven't touched a drop of alcohol since the invention of the funnel.
—*Malachy McCourt*

A productive drunk is the bane of moralists.
—*Anonymous*

Come quickly; I am tasting stars!
—*Dom Pérignon*
(1638–1715)
(At the discovery of champagne)

I'd take a Bromo, but I can't stand the noise.
—*W.C. Fields*

The worst thing about some men is that when they are not drunk they are sober.
—*William Butler Yeats*
(1865–1939)

An Irishman is not drunk as long as he still has a blade of grass to hang onto.
—*Anonymous*

An alcoholic is someone you don't like who drinks as much as you do.
—*Dylan Thomas*
(1914–1953)

117

I can't die until the government finds a safe place to bury my liver.
—*Phil Harris*

My uncle was the town drunk—and we lived in Chicago.
—*George Gobel*

Somebody left the cork out of my lunch.
—*W.C. Fields*

I have to think hard to name an interesting man who does not drink.
—*Richard Burton*

Reality is a crutch for people who can't cope with drugs.
—*Lily Tomlin*

I never took hallucinogenic drugs because I never wanted my consciousness expanded one unnecessary iota.
—*Fran Lebowitz*

The government announced today that there may be some medical benefits to marijuana. Does this mean that the Grateful Dead have a better health plan than President Clinton?
—*Jay Leno*

The U.S. Army announced today that it was true that during the first part of the nineteen sixties they had performed LSD experiments on human beings and destroyed their minds. However, they claim that none of the victims has been promoted beyond Lieutenant Colonel.
—*George Carlin*

A cap of good acid costs five dollars and for that you can hear the Universal Symphony with God singing solo and the Holy Ghost on drums.
—*Hunter S. Thompson*

There are three side effects of acid. Enhanced long-term memory, decreased short–term memory and I forget the third.
—*Timothy Leary*

ADVICE

Advice is seldom welcome; and those who want it the most always like it the least.
—*Earl of Chesterfield*

There is no human problem which could not be solved if people would simply do as I advise.
—*Gore Vidal*

Good advice is one of those insults that ought to be forgiven.
—*Anonymous*

Advice is like kissing. It costs nothing and is a pleasant thing to do.
—H.W. Shaw

We hate to have some people give us advice because we know how badly they need it themselves. *—Laurence J. Peter*

If someone gives you so-called good advice, do the opposite; you can be sure it will be the right thing nine out of ten times.
—Anselm Feuerbach
(1829–1880)

I have found the best way to give advice to your children is to find out what they want and then advise them to do it.
—Harry S Truman

The odds against there being a bomb on a plane are a million to one, and against two bombs a million times a million to one. Next time you fly, cut your odds and take a bomb. *—Benny Hill*

Never try to walk across a river just because it has an average depth of four feet. *—Martin Friedman*

Never get deeply in debt to someone who cried at the end of Scarface. *—Robert S. Wieder*

Open your mouth only to change feet. *—Stanley Ralph Ross*

The squeaking wheel doesn't always get the grease. Sometimes it gets replaced. *—Vic Gold*

Live in such a way that you would not be ashamed to sell your parrot to the town gossip. *—Will Rogers*

When you get to the end of your rope, tie a knot and hang on. And swing! *—Leo Buscaglia*

Start by doing what's necessary, then what's possible and suddenly you are doing the impossible. *—St. Francis of Assisi*

Talk low, talk slow and don't say too much. *—John Wayne*

Learn from the mistakes of others—you can never live long enough to make them all yourself. *—Anonymous*

Always do what you are afraid to do. *—Ralph Waldo Emerson*

Always look out for Number One and be careful not to step in Number Two. *—Rodney Dangerfield*

Never go to sea with two chronometers; take one or three.
—Anonymous

Arguments are to be avoided; they are always vulgar and often convincing. *—Oscar Wilde*
(1854–1900)

CYNICISM & LOGIC

A cynic is a person searching for an honest man, with a stolen lamp.
—Edgar A. Shoaff

Cynic *n* : a blackguard whose faulty vision sees things as they are, not as they ought to be. *—Ambrose Bierce*
(1842–1914)

Cynicism is an unpleasant way of saying the truth.
—Lillian Hellman

The power of accurate observation is commonly called cynicism by those who have not got it. *—George Bernard Shaw*

Cynicism is knowing the price of everything and the value of nothing. *—Oscar Wilde*
(1854–1900)

A cynic is a man who, when he smells flowers, looks around for a coffin. *—H.L. Mencken*
(1880–1956)

Logic is a system whereby one may go wrong with confidence.
—Charles Kettering

Against logic there is no armor like ignorance.   *—Laurence J. Peter*

We live in a Newtonian world of Einsteinian physics ruled by Frankenstein logic. *—David Russell*

"Contrariwise," continued Tweedledee, "If it was so, it might be; and if it were so, it would be; but as it isn't, it ain't. That's logic."
—Lewis Carroll
(Charles Lutwidge Dodgson)

MONEY

I have enough money to last me the rest of my life, unless I buy something.
—Jackie Mason

I don't know much about being a millionaire, but I'll bet I'd be darling at it.
—Dorothy Parker

Tradition is what you resort to when you don't have the time or the money to do it right.
—Kurt Herbert Adler

Whoever said money can't buy happiness didn't know where to shop.
—Anonymous

Behind every great fortune there is a crime.
—Honoré de Balzac
(1799–1850)

If Women didn't exist, all the money in the world would have no meaning.
—Aristotle Onassis
(1906–1975)

Save a little money each month and at the end of the year you'll be surprised at how little you have.
—Ernest Haskins

My problem lies in reconciling my gross habits with my net income.
—Errol Flynn
(1909–1959)

Any man who has $10,000 left when he dies is a failure.
—Errol Flynn
(1909–1959)

I'm living so far beyond my income that we may almost be said to be living apart.
—e e cummings
(1894–1962)

I don't like money, but it quiets my nerves.
—Joe Lewis
(1914–1981)

Money can't buy friends, but it can get you a better class of enemy.
—Spike Milligan

The rule is not to talk about money with people who have much more or much less than you.
—Katherine Whitehorn

The way to make money is to buy when blood is running in the streets.
—John D. Rockefeller

The upper crust is a bunch of crumbs held together by dough.
—Joseph A. Thomas
(1906–1977)

What some people mistake for the high cost of living is really the cost of high living. *—Doug Larson*

Capital is only the fruit of labor, and could not have existed if labor had not first existed. *—Abraham Lincoln*

The only sure way to double your money is to fold it and put it in your pocket. *—Anonymous*

Money frees you from doing things you dislike. Since I dislike doing nearly everything, money is handy. *—Groucho Marx*

If you don't want to work, you have to work to earn enough money so that you won't have to work. *—Ogden Nash*
(1902–1971)

It is morally wrong to allow suckers to keep their money.
—Canada Bill Jones

A man must properly pay the fiddler. In my case it so happened that a whole symphony orchestra had to be subsidized. *—John Barrymore*

All progress is based upon a universal innate desire on the part of every organism to live beyond its income. *—Samuel Butler*

Every morning I get up and look through the Forbes list of the richest people in America. If I'm not there, I go to work. *—Robert Orben*

We're overpaying him, but he's worth it. *—Samuel Goldwyn*

The hard part of being broke is watching the rest of the world go buy. *—Alan F.G. Lewis*

WAR & CONFLICT

I propose getting rid of conventional armaments and replacing them with reasonably priced hydrogen bombs that would be distributed equally throughout the world. *—Idi Amin*

I thoroughly disapprove of duels. If a man should challenge me, I would take him kindly and forgivingly by the hand and lead him to a quiet place and kill him. *—Mark Twain*

There is nothing more exhilarating than to be shot at without result.
—*Winston Churchill*
(1874–1965)

On my travels to just about every part of this earth, I've landed on asphalt, grass, mud—and a wing and a prayer. I've been welcomed with "Aloha," "Shalom," "Wilkommen," "Benvenuto" and a 21–gun salute—which fortunately missed.
—*Bob Hope*

Cannon *n* : An instrument employed in the rectification of national boundaries.
—*Ambrose Bierce*
(1842–1914)

War is a series of catastrophes that results in a victory.
—*Georges Clemenceau*
(1841–1929)

You can no more win a war than you can win an earthquake.
—*Jeannette Rankin*
(1880–1973)

I'd like to see the government get out of war altogether and leave the whole field to private industry.
—*Joseph Heller*

Name me an emperor who was ever struck by a cannonball.
—*Emperor Charles V*
(1500–1558)

I have already given two cousins to the war and I stand ready to sacrifice my wife's brother.
—*Artemus Ward*
(1834–1867)

Join the army, see the world, meet interesting people and kill them.
—*Anonymous*

Being in the army is like being in the Boy Scouts, except that the Boy Scouts have adult supervision.
—*Blake Clark*

War is the unfolding of miscalculations.
—*Barbara Tuchman*
(1912–1989)

A doctor could make a million dollars if he could figure out a way to bring a boy into the world without a trigger finger.
—*Arthur Miller*

Peace *n* : In international affairs, a period of cheating between two periods of fighting.
—*Ambrose Bierce*
(1842–1914)

As far as Saddam Hussein being a great military strategist, he is neither a strategist, nor is he schooled in the operational arts, nor is he
a tactician, nor is he a general, nor is he a soldier. Other than that,
he's a great military man. I want you to know that.

—*General H. Norman Schwarzkopf*

You can't say civilizations don't advance . . . in every war they kill you
in a new way. —*Will Rogers*

It's always sad when a 10-year old gets drawn into a war.

—*Matt Groening*
(Creator of "The Simpsons,"
commenting on a photo of
Secretary of Defense Dick Cheney
holding a Bart Simpson doll
dressed in camouflage)

A revolution is a violent change of mismanagement.

—*Ambrose Bierce*
(1842–1914)

They must think it's the food of choice of the American plutocracy.

—*Gustavo Gorriti*
(Peruvian journalist,
on two rebel bombings of Lima
Kentucky Fried Chicken outlets)

Never go to bed mad. Stay up and fight. —*Phyllis Diller*

Truce is better than friction. —*Charles Herguth*

Nobody ever forgets where he buried the hatchet. —*Kin Hubbard*

I do not want people to be agreeable, as it saves me the trouble of lik-
ing them. —*Jane Austen*

I'm free of all prejudices. I hate everyone equally. —*W.C. Fields*

The best remedy for a short temper is a long walk.

—*Jacqueline Schiff*

A man can't be too careful in the choice of his enemies.

—*Oscar Wilde*
(1854–1900)

NATURE & ANIMALS

The reason lightning doesn't strike twice in the same place is that the same place isn't there the second time.   *—Willie Tyler*

A February thaw is merely nature's way of warning us against overoptimism.   *—Bill Vaughan*

A lot of people like snow. I find it to be an unnecessary freezing of water.   *—Carl Reiner*

I hate the outdoors. To me the outdoors is where the car is.
—Will Durst

Never does nature say one thing and wisdom another.   *—Juvenal (60?–140)*

Nature is wonderful. A million years ago she didn't know we were going to need glasses, but look where she put our ears.
—Los Angeles Times Syndicate

Really, we create nothing. We merely plagiarize nature.
—Jean Bataillon

The trouble with dawn is that it comes too early in the day.
—Susan Richman

The early worm gets caught.   *—John Igo*

Birds of a feather flock to a newly washed car.   *—Marlys Bradley*

In a better-ordered world, the gypsy moth would show up in October and eat the leaves after they've fallen.   *—Edward Stevenson*

Armadillo—Possum on the half-shell.   *—Lewis Grizzard*

Cats are like Baptists. They raise hell but you can't catch them at it.
—Anonymous

It took me an hour to bury the cat. It wouldn't stop moving.
—Monty Python

A man who was loved by 300 women singled me out to live with him. Why? I was the only one without a cat.   *—Elayne Boosler*

If Darwin's theory of evolution was correct, cats would be able to operate a can opener by now.   *—Larry Wright*

If the English language made any sense, a catastrophe would be an apostrophe with fur.   *—Doug Larson*

Curiosity killed the cat, but for a while I was a suspect.
>—*Steven Wright*

For a well-balanced perspective, the person who has a dog to worship him should also have a cat to ignore him.
>—*The Peterborough (Ontario)* Examiner

Women and cats do as they damned well please. Men and dogs had best learn to live with it.
>—*Alan Holbrook*

Cats are smarter than dogs. You can't get eight cats to pull a sled through snow.
>—*Jeff Valdez*

Dogs come when they're called; cats take a message and get back to you.
>—*Mary Bly*

I like pigs. Dogs look up to us. Cats look down on us. Pigs treat us as equals.
>—*Winston Churchill*
>*(1874–1965)*

To his dog, every man is Napoléon Bonaparte; hence the constant popularity of dogs.
>—*Aldous Huxley*

No matter how eloquently a dog may bark, he cannot tell you that his parents were poor but honest.
>—*Bertrand Russell*

I take my pet lion to church every Sunday. He has to eat.
>—*Marty Pollio*

The groundhog is like most other prophets; it delivers its prediction and then disappears.
>—*Bill Vaughan*

You can lead a horse to water, but you can't make him float.
>—*Anonymous*

The horse is an eight-year-old gelding trained by the owner who races him with his wife.
>—*New Zealand* Times

PRODUCTIVE WORK & OTHER OXYMORONIC PASTIMES

GOVERNMENT & POLITICIANS

It's said that power corrupts, but actually it's more true that power attracts the corruptible. The sane are usually attracted by other things than power.
—David Brin

Political history is far too criminal a subject to be a fit thing to teach children.
—W.H. Auden
(1907–1973)

I think the world is run by 'C' students.
—Al McGuire

Could the legislature please vote a mandatory three-month sentence for people who, after they're told they dialed the wrong number, abruptly hang up?
—Mark Patinkin

Being in politics is like being a football coach. You have to be smart enough to understand the game, and dumb enough to think it's important.
—Eugene McCarthy

It could probably be shown by facts and figures that there is no distinctively native American criminal class except Congress.
—Mark Twain

In America any boy may become President. I suppose that's just one of the risks he takes.
—Adlai Stevenson

A statesman is a successful politician who is dead.
—Thomas B. Reed

A statesman is a dead politician. Lord knows we need more statesmen.
—Berke Breathed

Jello—An edible substance best comprehended as having the taste of a politician's promises and the consistency of his spine; sweet, but nonexistent.
—Gordon Bowker

Atrophy is a reward for long political service.
—Alan F.G. Lewis

When I was a boy I was told that anybody could become President. I'm beginning to believe it.
—Clarence Darrow
(1857–1938)

It is inaccurate to say I hate everything. I am strongly in favor of common sense, common honesty and common decency. This makes me forever ineligible for any public office. —*H.L. Mencken*
(1880–1956)

What this country needs is more unemployed politicians.
—*Edward Langley*

Man is the only animal that laughs and has a state legislature.
—*Samuel Butler*
(1835–1902)

Ninety-eight percent of the adults in this country are decent, hard-working, honest Americans. It's the other lousy two percent that get all the publicity. But then—we elected them. —*Lily Tomlin*

All the men on my staff can type. —*Bella Abzug*

The man with the best job in the country is the Vice President. All he has to do is get up every morning and say, "How's the President?"
—*Will Rogers*

Every decent man is ashamed of the government he lives under.
—*H.L. Mencken*
(1880–1956)

If voting changed anything, they'd make it illegal. —*Anonymous*

Vote early and vote often. —*Al Capone*
(1899–1947)

Ninety percent of the politicians give the other ten percent a bad reputation. —*Henry Kissinger*

I might have gone to West Point, but I was too proud to speak to a congressman. —*Will Rogers*

Politics is a means of preventing people from taking part in what properly concerns them. —*Paul Valéry*
(1871–1945)

Politics consists of choosing between the disastrous and the unpalatable. —*John Kenneth Galbraith*

There has never been a good government. —*Emma Goldman*
(1869–1940)

A politician can appear to have his nose to the grindstone while strad-dling a fence and keeping both ears to the ground.   —*Anonymous*

No matter what your religion, you should try to become a govern-ment program, for then you will have everlasting life.
                                        —*Congresswoman Lynn Martin*

Early today the senator called a spade a spade. He later issued a retraction.   —*Joe Mirachi*

Voters want a fraud they can believe in.   —*Will Durst*

Are the people who run for president really the best in a country of 240 million? If so, something has happened to the gene pool.
                                        —*Bob McKenzie*

Tomorrow is Labor Day, I suppose set by act of Congress. How Congress knows anything about labor is beyond me.   —*Will Rogers*

The only thing the United States Senate agreed on this summer was to cut off the funds for the Library of Congress to be used for print-ing Playboy magazine in Braille. Leadership at last from our fearless lawmakers. What to do about pornography? Take it away from blind people, the only people who really read the articles.   —*Mark Russell*

If politicians and scientists were lazier, how much happier we should all be.   —*Evelyn Waugh*
                                        (1903–1966)

There is but one way for a newspaperman to look at a politician and that is down.   —*Frank H. Simonds*
                                        (1878–1936)

The reason there are so few female politicians is that it is too much trouble to put makeup on two faces.   —*Maureen Murphy*

An honest politician is one who when he is bought will stay bought.
                                        —*Simon Cameron*
                                        (1799–1889)

Too bad the only people who know how to run the country are busy driving cabs and cutting hair.   —*George Burns*

Those who are too smart to engage in politics are punished by being governed by those who are dumber.   —*Plato*
                                        (427?–348? B.C.)

It's the responsibility of the media to look at the president with a microscope, but they go too far when they use a proctoscope.
—Richard M. Nixon

When we got into office, the thing that surprised me the most was that things were as bad as we'd been saying they were.
—John F. Kennedy
(1917–1963)

A lot of people think the country is going to hell and guys like me are leading us there. I'm no shoo-in.   *—Phil Donahue*
(Assessing his chances of
being elected to Congress)

The Constitution gives every American the inalienable right to make a damn fool of himself.   *—John Ciardi*

A reformer is a guy who rides through a sewer in a glass-bottomed boat.   *—Jimmy Walker*

This country will not be a good place for any of us to live in unless we make it a good place for all of us to live in.   *—Theodore Roosevelt*

This land of ours cannot be a good place for any of us to live in unless it is a good place for all of us to live in.   *—Richard M. Nixon*

What should be done to give power into the hands of capable and well-meaning persons has so far resisted all efforts.
—Albert Einstein

I once said cynically of a politician, "He'll doublecross that bridge when he comes to it."   *—Oscar Levant*

Politicians are the same all over. They promise to build bridges even where there are no rivers.   *—Nikita Khrushchev*

Politicians should read science fiction, not westerns and detective stories.   *—Arthur C. Clarke*

Politics is not the art of the possible. It consists of choosing between the disastrous and the unpalatable.   *—John Kenneth Galbraith*

Since a politician never believes what he says, he is surprised when others believe him.   *—Charles de Gaulle*

The trouble with the profit system has always been that it was highly unprofitable to most people.   *—E.B. White*

The government is unresponsive to the needs of the little man.
Under 5'7", it is impossible to get your congressman on the phone.

—*Woody Allen*

You couldn't get the Ten Commandments through Congress if
Moses was buying drinks.   —*Gallagher*

I never vote for anyone; I always vote against.   —*W.C. Fields*

Almost all reformers, however strict their social conscience, live in
houses just as big as they can pay for.   —*Logan Pearsall Smith*

If living conditions don't stop improving in this country, we're going
to run out of humble beginnings for our great men.

—*Russell P. Askue*

Why does a slight tax increase cost you $200 and a substantial tax cut
save you 30 cents?   —*Peg Bracken*

I can't understand what's holding up our missile program. It's the
first time the government ever had trouble making the taxpayers'
money go up in smoke.   —*Bob Hope*

There is no kind of dishonesty into which otherwise good people
more easily and frequently fall than that of defrauding the government.   —*Benjamin Franklin*
          (1706–1790)

We have taxed our economy the way old-time doctors bled their
patients, and with similar results.

—*Massachusetts Gov. William Weld*
(Inaugural address)

One thing the world needs is popular government at popular prices.

—*George Barker*

There is one difference between a tax collector and a taxidermist; the
taxidermist leaves the hide.   —*Mortimer Caplin*

Did you ever get to wondering if taxation without representation
might have been cheaper?   —*Robert Orben*

Taxation with representation ain't so hot, either.   —*Gerald Barzan*

A billion here, a billion there—pretty soon it adds up to real money.
—*Senator Everett Dirksen*
(1896–1969)

There is very little to admire in bureaucracy, but you have to hand it to the Internal Revenue Service.   *—James L. Rogers*

The income tax has made liars out of more Americans than golf.
—Will Rogers

Bureaucracy is based on a willingness either to pass the buck or spend it.   *—Mrs. Henry J. Serwat*

The only thing that saves us from the bureaucracy is its inefficiency.
—Eugene McCarthy

Guidelines for Bureaucrats:
  (1) When in charge ponder
  (2) When in trouble delegate.
  (3) When in doubt mumble.   *—James H. Boren*

Bureaucracy defends the status quo long past the time when the quo has lost its status.   *—Laurence J. Peter*

Diplomacy *n* : The patriotic art of lying for one's country.
—Ambrose Bierce
(1842–1914)

Diplomacy is the art of letting someone else have your way.
—Anonymous

An ambassador is an honest man sent abroad to lie for his country.
—Sir Henry Wotton
(1568–1639)

It's not the voting that's democracy; it's the counting.
—Tom Stoppard

Diplomacy is the art of saying "Nice doggie" until you can find a rock.   *—Will Rogers*

Fanaticism consists of redoubling your effort when you have forgotten your aim.   *—George Santayana*
(1863–1952)

All movements go too far.   *—Bertrand Russell*

Get all the fools on your side and you can be elected to anything.
—Frank Dane

It is dangerous to be right when the government is wrong.
—Voltaire

Change means movement, movement means friction, friction means heat, and heat means controversy. The only place where there is no friction is in outer space or a seminar on political action.

—*Saul Alinsky*

The radical of one century is the conservative of the next. The radical invents the views. When he has worn them out the conservative adopts them. —*Mark Twain*

Democracy is the art of running the circus from the monkey cage.
—*H.L. Mencken*
(1880–1956)

Communism is like one big phone company. —*Lenny Bruce*

Democracy is the theory that the common people know what they want, and deserve to get it good and hard. —*H.L. Mencken*
(1880–1956)

Democracy gives every man the right to be his own oppressor.
—*James Russell Lowell*

It has been said that democracy is the worst form of government except all the others that have been tried. —*Winston Churchill*
(1874–1965)

Democracy is being allowed to vote for the candidate you dislike least. —*Robert Byrne*

Democracy substitutes election by the incompetent many for appointment by the corrupt few. —*George Bernard Shaw*

The function of socialism is to raise suffering to a higher level.
—*Norman Mailer*

Under capitalism man exploits man; under socialism the reverse is true. —*Polish proverb*

Politically I believe in democracy, but culturally, not at all. Whenever a cultural matter rolls up a majority, I know it is wrong.
—*John Sloan*

The Communist system must be based on the will of the people, and if the people should not want that system, then that people should establish a different system. —*Nikita S. Khrushchev*

The inherent vice of capitalism is the unequal sharing of blessings; the inherent virtue of socialism is the equal sharing of miseries.

—*Winston Churchill*
(1874–1965)

They cannot lead, they will not follow, and they refuse to cooperate.

—*Harold Ickes*

Nixon, Ford, Carter and Reagan—a Mount Rushmore of incompetence.

—*David Steinberg*

Now you take, for instance, a Republican. There's a lot of people that won't speak or associate with one. They think they would catch some grafting disease, but I have met several of them and you take one, when he is out of office, and he is as nice a fellow as you would want to meet.

—*Will Rogers*

Hell hath no fury like a liberal scorned.

—*Dick Gregory*

You have to be a Republican to know how good it is to be a Democrat.

—*Jacqueline Kennedy Onassis*

How did sex come to be thought of as dirty in the first place? God must have been a Republican.

—*Will Durst*

My grandmother's brain was dead, but her heart was still beating. It was the first time we ever had a Democrat in the family.

—*Emo Phillips*

There was a lady that passed away the other day in Indiana, and she had been a lifelong Democrat. She asked to be buried in Chicago so she could stay active in party politics.

—*Mark Russell*

If the Republicans will stop telling lies about the Democrats, we will stop telling the truth about them.

—*Adlai Stevenson*

At the political conventions of 1992 the Democrats were terminally smug, while the Republicans managed to rise to the challenges of 1957.

—*Mark Russell*

A conservative is a man who wants the rules changed so that no one can make a pile the way he did.

—*Gregory Nunn*

Liberals feel unworthy of their possessions. Conservatives feel they deserve everything they've stolen.

—*Mort Sahl*

A conservative doesn't want anything to happen for the first time; a liberal feels it should happen, but not now.

—*Mort Sahl*

Conservative *n* : A statesman who is enamored of existing evils, as distinguished from the liberal, who wishes to replace them with others.
—Ambrose Bierce
(1842–1914)

A liberal is a conservative who's been arrested.　　　*—Tom Wolfe*

A conservative is a man who is too cowardly to fight and too fat to run.
—Elbert Hubbard

Conservatives are not necessarily stupid, but most stupid people are conservatives.
—John Stuart Mill
(1806–1873)

A conservative is a man who does not think that anything should be done for the first time.
—Frank Vanderlip

A conservative is like a player trying to steal second base while keeping his foot on first.
—Laurence J. Peter

JUSTICE & ATTORNEYS

The law, in its majestic equality, forbids the rich as well as the poor, to sleep under bridges, to beg in the streets and to steal bread.
—Anatole France

Two farmers each claimed to own a certain cow. While one pulled on its head and the other pulled on its tail, the cow was milked by a lawyer.
—Jewish proverb

It is better to be a mouse in a cat's mouth than a man in a lawyer's hands.
—Spanish proverb

A citizen may snore with immunity in his own home, even though he may be in possession of unusual and exceptional ability in that particular field.
—From a Los Angeles judge's ruling

Lawsuit *n* : A machine you go into as a pig and come out of as a sausage.
—Ambrose Bierce
(1842–1914)

Laws are like sausages. It's better not to see them being made.
—Otto von Bismarck
(1815–1898)

Agree, for the law is costly.　　　*—William Camden*

How to win a case in court: If the law is on your side, pound on the law; if the facts are on your side, pound on the facts; if neither is on your side, pound on the table. *—Anonymous*

Nobody wants justice. *—Alan Dershowitz*

Justice is incidental to law and order. *—J. Edgar Hoover*

Injustice is relatively easy to bear; what stings is justice.
—H.L. Mencken
(1880–1956)

Justice is when the decision is in our favor *—Laurence J. Peter*

Go not in and out of court that thy name may not stink.
—The Wisdom of Anii
(c.900 B.C.)

When men are pure, laws are useless; when men are corrupt, laws are broken. *—Benjamin Disraeli*
(1804–1881)

A jury consists of twelve persons chosen to decide who has the better lawyer. *—Robert Frost*

Jury—A group of twelve men who, having lied to the judge about their hearing, health and business engagements, have failed to fool him. *—H.L. Mencken*
(1880–1956)

When you go into court you are putting your fate into the hands of twelve people who weren't smart enough to get out of jury duty.
—Norm Crosby

Courtroom—A place where Jesus Christ and Judas Iscariot would be equals, with the betting odds in favor of Judas. *—H.L. Mencken*
(1880–1956)

Nobody outside of a baby carriage or a judge's chamber believes in an unprejudiced point of view. *—Lillian Hellman*
(1907–1984)

Talk is cheap until you hire a lawyer. *—Anonymous*

Correction—the following typo appeared in our last bulletin: "Lunch will be gin at 12:15." Please correct to read "12 noon."
—California Bar Association Bulletin

136

Imagine the appeals,
Dissents and remandments,
If lawyers had written
The Ten Commandments.   —*Harry Bender*

A countryman between two lawyers is like a fish between two cats.
    —*Benjamin Franklin*

Lawyers, I suppose, were children once.   —*Charles Lamb*
    (1775–1834)

Getting kicked out of the American Bar Association is like getting
kicked out of the Book-of-the-Month Club.   —*Melvin Belli*

You cannot fling a brick in this city without hitting a water lawyer,
which strikes some people as a good reason for brick-flinging.
    George Will
    (Referring to Denver)

Valentine's Day is a great time to serve someone a summons. You
put it in flowers. Everyone accepts flowers. I tell my clients, be a
sport. Go for a dozen roses. Do it with style.   —*Jaclyn Barnett*
    Manhattan lawyer

The first thing we do, let's kill all the lawyers.
    —*William Shakespeare*
    Henry VI, Part 2

A lawyer is a man who helps you get what is coming to him.
    —*Laurence J. Peter*

You're an attorney. It's your duty to lie, conceal and distort everything, and slander everybody.   —*Jean Giraudoux*

The minute you read something you can't understand, you can
almost be sure it was drawn up by a lawyer.   —*Will Rogers*

Lawyers spend a great deal of their time shoveling smoke.
    —*Oliver W. Holmes, Jr*

If law school is so hard to get through . . . how come there are so
many lawyers?   —*Calvin Trillin*

Death is not the end; there remains the litigation.   —*Ambrose Bierce*
    (1842–1914)

HEALING & DOCTORS

The art of medicine consists of amusing the patient while nature cures the disease.
—Voltaire
(1694–1778)

The art of medicine, like that of war, is murderous and conjectural.
—Voltaire
(1694—1778)

My plastic surgeon told me my face looked like a bouquet of elbows.
—Phyllis Diller

A young doctor means a new graveyard.
—German proverb

My doctor gave me two weeks to live. I hope they're in August.
—Ronnie Shakes

When I told my doctor I couldn't afford an operation, he offered to touch-up my X-rays.
—Henny Youngman

Your medical tests are in. You're short, fat and bald.
—Tom Wilson

We Americans live in a nation where the medical–care system is second to none in the world, unless you count maybe 25 or 30 scuzzball countries like Scotland that we could vaporize in seconds if we felt like it.
—Dave Barry

Do you realize that somewhere in the world is the worst doctor. Has to be. Process of elimination. Sooner or later you are going to find the worst doctor. The weird part is someone has an appointment tomorrow.
—George Carlin

A male gynecologist is like an auto mechanic who has never owned a car.
—Carrie Snow

The patient is not likely to recover who makes the doctor his heir.
—Thomas Fuller
(1608–1661)

I'm going to Boston to see my doctor. He's a very sick man.
—Fred Allen

A doctor's reputation is made by the number of eminent men who die under his care.
—George Bernard Shaw

A hospital is no place to be sick.
—Samuel Goldwyn

If I were a medical man, I should prescribe a holiday to any patient who considered his work important. —*Bertrand Russell*

She got her good looks from her father. He's a plastic surgeon.
—*Groucho Marx*

A rule of thumb in the matter of medical advice is to take everything any doctor says with a grain of aspirin. —*Goodman Ace*
(1899–1982)

PSYCHOANALYSIS

There is an old saying; "Neurotics build castles in the air and psychotics live in them." My mother cleans them. —*Rita Rudner*

Sometimes a cigar is just a cigar. —*Sigmund Freud*

Psychiatry—The art of claiming to be able to cure those who are strung up, practiced by one who deserves to be. —*Gordon Bowker*

Psychiatry enables us to correct our faults by confessing our parents' shortcomings. —*Laurence J. Peter*

I quit therapy because my analyst was trying to help me behind my back. —*Richard Lewis*

The closest I've gotten to a ménage-à-trois was dating a schizophrenic. —*Rita Rudner*

Behavioral psychology is the science of pulling habits out of rats.
—*Dr. Douglas Busch*

Anyone who goes to a psychiatrist ought to have his head examined.
—*Samuel Goldwyn*

I'm going to give my psychoanalyst one more year, then I'm going to Lourdes. —*Woody Allen*

After twelve years of therapy my psychiatrist said something that brought tears to my eyes. He said, "*No hablo inglés.*"
—*Ronnie Shakes*

After a year in therapy, my psychiatrist said to me, "Maybe life isn't for everyone." —*Larry Brown*

Half of analysis is anal. —*Marty Indik*

Why should I tolerate a perfect stranger at the bedside of my mind?
—*Vladimir Nabokov*
(1899–1977)

Show me a sane man and I will cure him for you.　　　—*Carl Jung*
(1875–1961)

Psychiatry is the care of the id by the odd.　　　—*Anonymous*

FINANCE & BANKERS

Finance is the art of passing money from hand to hand until it finally disappears.　　　—*Robert W. Sarnoff*

Gentlemen prefer bonds.　　　—*Andrew Mellon*
(1855–1937)

Whoever uses the term "dirt cheap" probably hasn't bought any real estate lately.　　　—*D.O. Flynn*

Easy payment plan: 100 percent down and no further payments.
—*Anonymous*

Pity the poor man who has a big load of debt and doesn't know how to budge it.　　　—*Alan F.G. Lewis*

The economy of Houston is so bad right now that two prostitutes the police arrested turned out to be virgins.　　　—*Bill Abeel*

To make a small fortune, invest a large fortune.　　　—*Bruce Cohn*

I had plastic surgery last week. I cut up my credit cards.
—*Henny Youngman*

A foundation is a large body of money surrounded by people who want some.　　　—*Dwight MacDonald*
(1906–1983)

The meek shall inherit the earth, but not the mineral rights.
—*J. Paul Getty*

Every man serves a useful purpose: A miser, for example, makes a wonderful ancestor.　　　—*Laurence J. Peter*

There's one thing worse than investing in a stock and seeing it plummet; deciding not to invest and seeing it skyrocket. —*Mark Patinkin*

A banker is a person who is willing to make a loan if you present sufficient evidence to show you don't need it.   —*Herbert V. Prochnow*

A banker is a fellow who lends you his umbrella when the sun is shining, but wants it back the minute it begins to rain.—*Mark Twain*
(1835–1910)

A bank is a place where they lend you an umbrella in fair weather and ask for it back when it begins to rain.   —*Robert Frost*

I don't have a bank account because I don't know my mother's maiden name.   —*Paula Poundstone*

EDUCATION, TEACHERS & COLLEGE

I don't give a damn for a man that can only spell a word one way.
—*Mark Twain*

Education *n* : that which discloses to the wise and disguises from the foolish their lack of understanding.   —*Ambrose Bierce*
(1842–1914)

If you think education is expensive, try ignorance.   —*Derek Bok*

Education is what survives when what has been learned has been forgotten.   —*B.F. Skinner*

I respect faith, but doubt is what gets you an education.
—*Wilson Mizner*

Creative minds always have been known to survive any kind of bad training.   —*Anna Freud*

Everybody who is incapable of learning has taken to teaching.
—*Oscar Wilde*
(1854–1900)

The learned are seldom pretty fellows, and in many cases their appearance tends to discourage a love of study in the young.
—*H.L. Mencken*
(1880–1956)

I have never let my schooling interfere with my education.
—Mark Twain

Men are born ignorant, not stupid; they are made stupid by education.
—Bertrand Russell

In the first place, God made idiots. That was for practice. Then he made school boards.
— Mark Twain

Smartness runs in my family. When I went to school I was so smart my teacher was in my class for five years.
—George Burns

Why do you listen to a shop teacher missing fingers? Would you listen to a home ec. teacher burned beyond recognition?
—Tim Allen

In high school I was voted "girl most likely to become a nun." That may not be too impressive to you now, it was quite an accomplishment at the Hebrew Academy.
—Rita Rudner

There is a very odd tradition in this country which dictates, especially around commencement time, that someone who is tottering downhill will be able to tell people walking uphill what is over the top of the hill.
—Alistair Cooke

As far as the laws of mathematics refer to reality, they are not certain; and as far as they are certain, they do not refer to reality.
—Albert Einstein

In business school classrooms they construct wonderful models of a nonworld.
—Peter Drucker

College isn't the place to go for ideas.
—Helen Keller

The chief value in going to college is that it's the only way to learn it really doesn't matter.
—George Edwin Howes

I was thrown out of college for cheating on the metaphysics exam; I looked into the soul of the boy next to me.
—Woody Allen

College Professor—One who talks in other people's sleep.
—Bergen Evans

Fathers send their sons to college either because they went to college or because they didn't.
—L.L. Henderson

American college students are like American colleges—each has half-dulled faculties.
—James Thurber

A university is what a college becomes when the faculty loses interest in students. —*John Ciardi*

Universities are designed for the convenience of the faculty, not for the convenience of the students. —*Adam Smith*

It takes me several days, after I get back to Boston, to realize that the reference "the president" refers to the president of Harvard and not to a minor official in Washington. —*Oliver Wendell Holmes, Jr.*

I'd rather entrust the government of the United States to the first 400 people listed in the Boston telephone directory than to the faculty of Harvard University. —*William F. Buckley, Jr.*

University politics are vicious precisely because the stakes are so small. —*Henry Kissinger*

Palm Springs University—more than one hundred degrees available. —*Anonymous*

BUSINESS & EXECUTIVES

A criminal is a person with predatory instincts without sufficient capital to form a corporation. —*Howard Scott*

They can't fire me; slaves have to be sold. —*Anonymous*

Thief—A businessman who does not issue receipts. —*Gordon Bowker*

Toots Shor's restaurant is so crowded nobody goes there anymore. —*Yogi Berra*

Nothing succeeds like the appearance of success. —*Christopher Lasch*

Clothes make the man. Naked people have little or no influence on society. —*Mark Twain (1835–1910)*

Formula for success: Rise early, work hard, strike oil. —*J. Paul Getty*

Nothing is illegal if a hundred businessmen decide to do it. —*Andrew Young*

143

Every successful person has had failures, but repeated failure is no guarantee of eventual success.
—*Anonymous*

It is impossible to make anything foolproof, because fools are so ingenious.
—*Anonymous*

So much of what we call management consists in making it difficult for people to work.
—*Peter Drucker*

When large numbers of men are unable to find work, unemployment results.
—*Calvin Coolidge*

The closest anyone ever comes to perfection is on the job-application form.
—*Anonymous*

I've been promoted to middle management. I never thought I'd sink so low.
—*Tim Gould*

No man ever listened himself out of a job.
—*Calvin Coolidge*

A career is a job that has gone on too long.
—*Jeff MacNelly*
"Shoe"

Tell your boss what you think of him, and the truth shall set you free.
—*Anonymous*

A holding company is a thing where you hand an accomplice the goods while the policeman searches you.
—*Will Rogers*

My mistake was buying stock in the company. Now I worry about the lousy work I'm turning out.
—*Marvin Townsend*

I can't stand this proliferation of paperwork. It's useless to fight the forms. You've got to kill the people producing them.
—*Vladimir Kabaidze*
General Director
Ivanovo Machine Building Works
in a speech to the Communist Party

Cost does indeed vary as the product of the number of men and the number of months. Progress does not. Hence the man-month as a unit of measuring the size of a job is a dangerous and deceptive myth ... The bearing of a child takes nine months, no matter how many women are assigned.
—*Frederick Brooks*
The Mythical Man-Month

144

For every problem there is a solution that is simple, neat, and wrong.
—*H.L. Mencken*
(1880–1956)

A verbal contract isn't worth the paper it's written on.
—*Samuel Goldwyn*

We've run into a couple of problems, but nothing minor.
—*Brenda Collier*

It used to be that people needed products to survive. Now products need people to survive.   —*Nicholas Johnson*

I think that maybe in every company today there is always at least one person who is going crazy slowly.   —*Joseph Heller*

Anything worth doing is worth doing frantically.   —*Jane Tower*

At least it's not something we can't replace.   —*Joseph Gold*
Marketing Manager
Ringling Brothers and Barnum & Bailey Circus
(After April Fool's Day thieves
stole two tons of elephant manure)

The only things that evolve by themselves in an organization are disorder, friction, and malperformance.   —*Peter Drucker*

Nobody talks more of free enterprise and competition and of the best man winning than the man who inherited his father's store or farm.
—*C. Wright Mills*

There are two times in a man's life when he should not speculate: when he can't afford it and when he can.   —*Mark Twain*

Job enrichment has been around for sixty years. It's been successful every time it has been tried, but industry is not interested.
—*Peter Drucker*

A satisfied customer—we should have him stuffed!   —*Basil Fawlty*

The virtues of hard work are extolled most loudly by people without calluses.   —*Doug Larson*

Neither function alone nor simplicity alone defines a good design.
—*Frederick Brooks*
The Mythical Man Month

Add little to little and there will be a big pile.   —*Ovid*

I know what needs to be done—but every time I try to tackle a technical problem some bloody fool wants me to make a decision about trucks—or telephones—or some damn thing.   —*Robert Heinlein*
The Man Who Sold the Moon

The user does not know what he wants until he sees what he gets.
—*Ed Yourdon*

Are you at the point where you don't have the time to find solutions to the problems that are taking up all your time???
—*Mark C. Davison*

Making duplicate copies and computer printouts of things no one wanted even one of in the first place is giving America a new sense of purpose.   —*Andy Rooney*

ADVERTISING

Advertising is the rattling of a stick inside a swill bucket.
—*George Orwell*
(1903–1950)

Advertising may be described as the science of arresting human intelligence long enough to get money from it.   —*Stephen Leacock*

The superior man understands what is right; the inferior man understands what will sell.   —*Confucius*
(c.551–479 B.C.)

Whenever you hear the word "save," it is usually the beginning of an advertisement designed to make you spend money.
—*René Pierre-Gosset*

Advertise—A form of prestidigitating by means of which a conjuror induces his audience to pick its own pocket under the impression that it is picking someone else's.   —*Gordon Bowker*

If advertising encourages people to live beyond their means, so does matrimony.   —*Bruce Barton*

Let advertisers spend the same amount of money improving their product that they do on advertising and they wouldn't have to advertise it.   —*Will Rogers*

Nothing's so apt to undermine your confidence in a product as knowing that the commercial selling it has been approved by the company that makes it. —*Franklin P. Adams*
(1881–1960)

Advertising has done more to cause the social unrest of the twentieth century than any other single factor. —*Clare Barnes, Jr.*

Advertising is the art of making whole lies out of half truths.
—*Edgar A. Shoaff*

Advertising is a valuable economic factor because it is the cheapest way of selling goods, particularly if the goods are worthless.
—*Sinclair Lewis*

Nothing modernizes a home so completely as an ad offering it for sale. —*Laurence J. Peter*

COMMITTEES/CONFERENCES/MEETINGS

A committee is a cul-de-sac down which ideas are lured and then quietly strangled. —*Sir Barnett Cocks*
(c.1907)

Committee—A group of men who individually can do nothing but as a group decide that nothing can be done. —*Fred Allen*

You'll find in no park or city
A monument to a committee.
—*Victoria Pasternak*

Committees have become so important nowadays that subcommittees have to be appointed to do the work. —*Laurence J. Peter*

Committee—A group of men who keep minutes and waste hours.
—*Milton Berle*

Putting a bunch of people to work on the same problem doesn't make them a team. —*Gerald M. Weinberg*
The Psychology of Computer Programming

PROFESSIONS

All professions are conspiracies against the laity.

—*George Bernard Shaw*

PERFORMERS

People performing mime in public should be subject to citizen's arrest on the theory that the normal First Amendment protection of free speech has, in effect, been waived by someone who has formally adopted a policy of not speaking. —*Calvin Trillin*

Prostitution, like acting, is being ruined by amateurs.

—*Alexander Woollcott*

Some of the greatest love affairs I've known involved one actor, unassisted. —*Wilson Mizner*

The important thing in acting is to be able to laugh and cry. If I have to cry, I think of my sex life. If I have to laugh, I think of my sex life.

—*Glenda Jackson*

I used to go out exclusively with actresses and other female impersonators. —*Mort Sahl*

I enjoy being a highly overpaid actor. —*Roger Moore*

Things are so bad on Broadway today an actor is lucky to be miscast.

—*George S. Kaufman*
(1889–1961)

Actresses will happen in the best regulated families.

—*Oliver Herford*
(1863–1935)

The dead actor requested in his will that his body be cremated and ten percent of his ashes thrown in his agent's face. —*Anonymous*

CENSORS & CENSORSHIP

A censor is a man who knows more than he thinks you ought to.

—*Laurence J. Peter*

I am going to introduce a resolution to have the Postmaster General stop reading dirty books and deliver the mail. —*Gail McGee*

148

A man walking at night...sees a light in the window and says, "A mother praying for the safe return of her boy." A second man sees the light and says, "Oh boy, hanky-panky going on up there!" The second man is a censor.
—*Goodman Ace*
(1899–1982)

Censorship, like charity, should begin at home; but, unlike charity, it should end there.
—*Clare Boothe Luce*

I never knew a girl who was ruined by a bad book.   —*Jimmy Walker*

Some people wouldn't read a book even if it were banned.
—*Laurence J. Peter*

There is no such thing as a moral or an immoral book. Books are well written or badly written.
—*Oscar Wilde*
(1854–1900)

The dirtiest book of all is the expurgated book.   —*Walt Whitman*
(1819–1892)

Nothing so needs reforming as other people's habits.
—*Mark Twain*

People who have what they want are fond of telling people who haven't what they want that they really don't want it.   —*Ogden Nash*
(1902–1971)

Assassination is the extreme form of censorship.
—*George Bernard Shaw*

CRITICS

Ask a writer what he thinks about critics and the answer you get is akin to asking a lamppost how it feels about dogs.
—*Bert Randolph Sugar*

Critics are like eunuchs in a harem. They're there every night, they see it done every night, the see how it should be done every night but they can't do it themselves.   —*Brendan Behan*

I am a critic—as essential to the theatre as ants to a picnic.
—*Joseph Mankiewicz*

A man is a critic when he cannot be an artist, in the same way that a man becomes an informer when he cannot be a soldier.
—*Gustave Flaubert*

149

No statue has ever been put up to a critic.
—Jean Sibelius
(1865–1957)

A critic is a man who knows the way but can't drive the car.
—Kenneth Tynan
(1927–1980)

A critic is a legless man who teaches running.   *—Channing Pollock*

Any reviewer who expresses rage and loathing for a novel is prepos-
terous. He or she is like a person who has put on full armor and
attacked a hot fudge sundae.   *—Kurt Vonnegut, Jr.*

The *New York Times* Book Review is alive with the sound of axes
grinding.   *—Gore Vidal*

A bad review is like baking a cake with all the best ingredients and
having someone sit on it.   *—Danielle Steele*

Criticism is prejudice made plausible.   *—H.L. Mencken*
(1880–1956)

I am sitting in the smallest room in the house. I have your review in
front of me. Soon it will be behind me.   *—Max Reger*
(1873–1916)

Criticism comes easier than craftsmanship.   *—Zeuxis*
(c.400 B.C.)

I love criticism just so long as it's unqualified praise.
—Noël Coward

It is the sort of play that gives failures a bad name.   *—Walter Kerr*

To call Richard Brautigan's poetry doggerel is an insult to the entire
canine world.   *—Lazlo Coakley*

Your manuscript is both good and original, but the part that is good
is not original and the part that is original is not good.
—Samuel Johnson
(1709–1784)

The covers of this book are too far apart.   *—Ambrose Bierce*
(1842–1914)
(In a book review)

Reading this book is like waiting for the first shoe to drop.
—Ralph Novak

I would like to recommend this film to those who can stay interested in Ronald Coleman's amnesia for two hours and who could, with pleasure, eat a bowl of Yardley's shaving soap before breakfast.

—*James Agee*

There is no law against composing music when one has no ideas whatsoever. The music of Wagner, therefore, is perfectly legal.

—The National, *Paris*
1850

Listening to the Fifth Symphony of Ralph Vaughan Williams is like staring at a cow for forty-five minutes.   —*Aaron Copland*

Wagner's music is better than it sounds.   —*Bill Nye*

The prelude to *Tristan and Isolde* sounded as if a bomb had fallen into a large music factory and had thrown all the notes into confusion.   —The Tribune, *Berlin*
1871

The prelude to *Tristan and Isolde* reminds me of the Italian painting of the martyr whose intestines are slowly being unwound from his body on a reel.   —*Eduard Hanslick*
(1825–1904)

Wagner drives the nail into your head with swinging hammer blows.

—*P.A. Fiorentino*
(1806–1864)

Mr. Love's idea of playing a he-man was to extend his chest three inches and then follow it slowly across the stage.   —*Heywood Broun*
(1888–1939)

ECONOMISTS

Ask five economists and you'll get five different explanations (six if one went to Harvard).   —*Edgar R. Fiedler*

For those of you who don't know, "economics" is from the Greek "economae," meaning worthless heap of donkey poop.

—*Ed Soloman*

Economists are people who work with numbers but who don't have the personality to be accountants.   —*Anonymous*

An economist's guess is liable to be as good as anybody else's.

—*Will Rogers*

Mathematics has given economics rigor, but, alas, also mortis.
—*Robert Heilbroner*

Isn't it strange? The same people who laugh at gypsy fortune-tellers take economists seriously.　　　　　　　　　　—*Anonymous*

If all economists were laid end to end, they would not reach a conclusion.　　　　　　　　　　　　　—*George Bernard Shaw*

EXPERTS

A specialist is one who knows everything about something and nothing about anything else.　　　　　　　　　—*Ambrose Bierce*
　　　　　　　　　　　　　　　　　　　　　(1842–1914)

The man we call a specialist today was formerly called a man with a one-track mind.　　　　　　　　　　　　—*Endre Balogh*

The more ignorant the authority, the more dogmatic it is. In the fields where no real knowledge is even possible, the authorities are the fiercest and most assured and punish non-belief with the severest of penalties.　　　　　　　　　　　　—*Abraham Myerson*

The expert is a person who avoids the small errors as he sweeps on to the grand fallacy.　　　　　　　　　　　—*Anonymous*

Always listen to experts. They'll tell you what can't be done and why. Then do it.　　　　　　　　　　　　—*Lazaru Long*

An expert is someone who knows some of the worst mistakes that can be made in his subject and how to avoid them.
—*Werner Heisenberg*

WRITERS OF ALL KINDS

The novelist, afraid his ideas may be foolish, slyly puts them in the mouth of some other fool and reserves the right to disavow them.
—*Diane Johnson*

As a novelist, I tell stories and people give me money. Then financial planners tell me stories and I give them money.
—*Martin Cruz Smith*

A detective digs around in the garbage of people's lives. A novelist invents people and then digs around in their garbage.　—*Joe Gores*

A good novel tells us the truth about its hero; but a bad novel tells us the truth about its author. —*G.K. Chesterton*

The only reason for being a professional writer is that you can't help it. —*Leo Rosten*

What an author likes to write most is his signature on the back of a check. —*Brendan Francis*

Why authors write I do not know. As well ask why a hen lays an egg or a cow stands patiently while a farmer burglarizes her.
—*H.L. Mencken*
(1880–1956)

Never let a domestic quarrel ruin a day's writing. If you can't start the next day fresh, get rid of your wife. —*Mario Puzo*

Writing is easy. All you do is stare at a blank sheet of paper until drops of blood form on your forehead. —*Gene Fowler*
(1890–1960)

If a writer has to rob his mother he will not hesitate; the "Ode on a Grecian Urn" is worth any number of old ladies.
—*William Faulkner*
(1897–1962)

I'm a lousy writer; a helluva lot of people have got lousy taste.
—*Grace Metalious*
(1924–1964)

I can write better than anybody who can write faster, and I can write faster than anybody who can write better. —*A.J. Liebling*
(1904–1963)

If you were a member of Jesse James' band and people asked you what you were, you wouldn't say, "Well, I'm a desperado." You'd say something like, "I work in banks," or "I've done some railroad work." It took me a long time just to say "I'm a writer." It's really embarrassing. —*Roy Blount, Jr.*

The cure for writer's cramp is writer's block. —*Inigo DeLeon*

Writers have two main problems. One is writer's block, when the words won't come at all, and the other is logorrhea, when the words come so fast that they can hardly get to the wastebasket in time.
—*Cecilia Bartholomew*

When writers refer to themselves as "we" and to the reader as "you," it's two against one   —*Judith Rascoe*

Most writers regard the truth as their most valuable possession, and therefore are most economical in its use.   —*Mark Twain*

Every author, however modest, keeps a most outrageous vanity chained like a madman in the padded cell of his breast.
                                        —*Logan Pearsall Smith*
                                              (1865–1946)

Authors are easy to get on with—if you like children.
                                            —*Michael Joseph*
                                              (1897–1958)

A painter can hang his pictures, but a writer can only hang himself.
                                           —*Edward Dahlberg*
                                              (1900–1977)

If the doctor told me I had only six minutes to live, I'd type a little faster.   —*Isaac Asimov*

Either a writer doesn't want to talk about his work, or he talks about it more than you want.   —*Anatole Broyard*

Writing is a profession in which you have to keep proving your talent to people who have none.   —*Jules Renard*

Those who can, do. Those who can't, write the instructions.
                                          —*Branhorst Knowles*

It is a mean thief or a successful author that plunders the dead.
                                           —*Austin O'Malley*
                                              (1858–1932)

The only good author is a dead author.   —*Patrick O'Connor*
                                                (editor)

As a writer, I realize, I am always struggling to get to the bottom of a mystery I am constantly in the process of creating.
                                          —*Michael Mewshaw*

If you can't annoy somebody, there's little point in writing.
                                            —*Kingsley Amis*

If poetry comes not as naturally as the leaves to a tree, it better not come at all.   —*John Keats*

If you give me six lines written by the most honest man, I will find something in them to hang him. *—Cardinal Richelieu*

The author of the *Iliad* is either Homer or, if not Homer, somebody else of the same name. *—Aldous Huxley*

The best way to become acquainted with a subject is to write a book about it. *—Benjamin Disraeli*

Writing free verse is like playing tennis with the net down.
—Robert Frost

There is nothing to writing. All you do is sit down at a typewriter and open a vein. *—Red Smith*

If I ever needed a brain transplant, I'd choose a sportswriter because I'd want a brain that had never been used. *—Norm Van Brocklin (1926–1983)*

All of us learn to write in the second grade. Most of us go on to greater things. *—Bobby Knight*

Being a newspaper columnist is like being married to a nymphomaniac. It's great for the first two weeks. *—Lewis Grizzard*

All newspaper editorial writers ever do is come down from the hills after the battle is over and shoot the wounded. *—Anonymous*

Quotations are a columnist's bullpen. Stealing someone else's words frequently spares the embarrassment of eating your own.
—Peter Anderson

Working as a journalist is exactly like being a wallflower at an orgy.
—Nora Ephron

Journalists are like whores; as high as their ideals may be, they still have to resort to tricks to make money. *—A. Cygni*

In Hollywood, writers are considered only the first draft of human beings. *—Frank Deford*

You call this a script? Give me a couple of 5,000-dollar-a-week writers and I'll write it myself. *—Joe Pasternak*

The relationship of editor to author is knife to throat. *—Anonymous*

Some editors are failed writers, but so are most writers.
—T.S. Eliot (1888–1965)

INDEX

Abeel, Bill, 140
Abel, Milt, 33
Abzug, Bella, 128
Ace, Goodman, 34, 40, 139, 149
Acuff, Roy, 16
Adamic, Louis, 24
Adams, Brooks, 112
Adams, Franklin P., 5, 12, 13, 25, 64, 73, 147
Adams, Joey, 41
Ade, George, 81
Adler, Kurt Herbert, 121
Agee, James, 151
Aldiss, Brian, 11
Aleichem, Shalom, 98
Alfonso the Wise, 108
Alinsky, Saul, 101, 133
Allen, Dennis, 68
Allen, Fred, 43, 61, 63, 64, 78, 79, 99, 102, 111, 138, 147
Allen, Gracie, 5
Allen, Hervey, 109
Allen, Kelly, 21
Allen, Tim, 42, 142
Allen, Woody, 5, 11, 13, 19, 21, 23, 26, 27, 29, 30, 32, 35, 36, 37, 38, 39, 46, 49, 55, 74, 77, 90, 108, 109, 131, 139, 142
Altito, Noélie, 25
Altrincham, Lord, 74
Alzado, Lyle, 67, 91
American proverb, 105
Amiel, Henri Frédéric, 111
Amin, Idi, 122
Amis, Kingsley, 110, 154
Amory, Cleveland, 8
Anderson, Peter, 155
Andersson, Kent G., 91
Anthony, Susan B., 44
Arab proverb, 105
Aristotle, 10, 65, 108
Armour, Richard, 20
Ashley, Elizabeth, 60
Asimov, Isaac, 80, 154
Askue, Russell P., 131
Astor, Lady Nancy, 55
Auchincloss, Louis, 18, 35
Auden, W.H., 91, 127
Austen, Jane, 50, 124
Bacall, Lauren, 90
Backus, Jim, 54
Bacon, Francis, 9
Bacon, Roger, 73
Baez, Joan, 59
Bagehot, Walter, 72
Bailey, Covert, 47
Bailey, James Montgomery, 9
Baker, Russell, 48, 62, 89
Ball, Lucille, 16
Balogh, Endre, 152
Banducci, Sue, 16

Bankhead, Tallulah, 33, 38, 39, 91
Banks, Dr. Murray, 24
Banks, Russell, 28
Barker, George, 131
Barker, Myra, 68
Barkley, Alben W., 116
Barnes, Clare, Jr., 147
Barnett, Jaclyn, 137
Barry, Dave, 61, 82, 84, 138
Barry, Lynda, 19
Barrymore, John, 20, 29, 44, 45, 100, 122
Bartholomew, Cecilia, 153
Barton, Bruce, 17, 146
Baruch, Bernard M., 15
Barzan, Gerald, 131
Bataillon, Jean, 125
Battista, O.A., 113
Beaverbrook, Lord, 70, 110
Becher, N.Z., 81
Beecham, Thomas, 44
Behan, Brendan, 91, 149
Belfast graffito, 28
Belli, Melvin, 91, 137
Belloc, Hilaire, 91
Bellow, Saul, 18, 42
Benchley, Robert, 8, 91
Bender, Harry, 137
Bennett, Dan, 50
Benny, Jack, 92
Berenson, Bernard, 53
Berger, Thomas, 10
Berle, Milton, 39, 101, 147
Berlioz, Hector, 28
Bernard, Claude, 68
Bernstein, Al, 9
Berra, Yogi, 82, 92, 143
Bhartrihari, 18, 42
Bickerstaffe, Isaac, 50
Bierce, Ambrose, 5, 23, 26, 39, 52, 58, 64, 107, 112, 116, 120, 123, 124, 132, 134, 137, 141, 150, 152
Billings, Josh, 27, 41, 115
Birrell, Augustine, 72
Bishop, Steven, 77
Blanche, Francis, 46
Blanshard, Brand, 68
Blount, Roy, Jr., 72, 153
Blues Brothers, 102
Bluestone, Ed, 34
Bly, Mary, 126
Bodenhein, Maxwell, 88
Bogan, Louise, 38
Bok, Derek, 141
Boliska, Al, 79
Bombeck, Erma, 11, 13, 47, 84
Bonaparte, Napoléon, 92, 100, 107, 109
Boosler, Elayne, 32, 42, 110, 125

Boren, James H., 114, 132
Borge, Victor, 76, 77
Borges, Jorge Luis, 92
Bouhours, Dominique, 30
Bouton, Jim, 15
Bowie, David, 92
Bowie, Louise, 22
Bowker, Gordon, 29, 30, 34, 36, 45, 59, 116, 127, 139, 143, 146
Bowman, Dr. Karl, 18
Bracken, John, 88
Bracken, Peg, 131
Bradbury, Malcolm, 36
Bradley, Marlys, 125
Brando, Christian, 27
Brandreth, Gyles, 109
Breathed, Berke, 127
Brecht, Bertolt, 49, 114
Brilliant, Ashleigh, 23, 50
Brin, David, 127
Brogan, W., 87
Brooke, H., 74
Brooks, Frederick, 81, 144, 145
Brooks, Mel, 105
Brophy, Brigid, 41
Broun, Heywood, 13, 74, 107, 151
Brown, A. Whitney, 48
Brown, Gene, 9
Brown, Larry, 38, 139
Brown, Norman O., 28
Brown, Rita Mae, 33
Broyard, Anatole, 7, 154
Bruce, Lenny, 8, 103, 110, 133
Brush, Stephanie, 60
Buchwald, Art, 86
Buckley, William F., Jr., 53, 143
Bukowski, Charles, 29
Bunker, Archie, 57
Bunyan, John, 46
Buono, Victor, 37, 114
Burgess, Gelett, 45
Burke, Leo J., 12
Burns, George, 15, 16, 26, 27, 31, 37, 46, 55, 56, 129, 142
Burton, Richard, 118
Buscaglia, Leo, 119
Busch, Dr. Douglas, 139
Butkus, Dick, 83
Butler, Samuel, 12, 21, 51, 72, 122, 128
Buxbaum, Martin, 14
Byrne, Robert, 7, 13, 29, 31, 36, 38, 47, 52, 59, 60, 69, 73, 115, 133
Cabell, James Branch, 23
Caen, Herb, 10, 14, 28, 48, 102, 110, 116
Caesar, Sid, 68
Cain, James M., 98
California Bar Association Bulletin, 136

Calvino, Italo, 75
Camden, William, 135
Cameron, Simon, 129
Camus, Albert, 65
Caplin, Mortimer, 131
Capone, Al, 128
Capp, Al, 70
Carey, Sandra, 52
Carlin, George, 15, 89, 118, 138
Carlyle, Thomas, 92
Carroll, Lewis, 111, 120
Carson, Johnny, 8, 26, 27, 36, 68, 79, 88, 92, 105, 109, 110
Carter, Hodding, 80
Carter, Lillian, 86
Carvey, Dana, 92
Castle, H., 89
Cato the Elder, 92
Catullus, 107
Cebrian, Katherine, 48
Chamberlain, Wilt, 92
Chambless, David, 19
Chamfort, Sébastien, 71, 104, 108
Chandler, Raymond, 31
Chapman, George, 65
Charles, Prince of Wales, 58, 103
Charles V (Emperor), 123
Chayevsky, Paddy, 78
Cher, 55
Chesterfield, Earl of, 9, 39, 55, 118
Chesterton, G.K., 47, 70, 153
Chevalier, Maurice, 20
Chicago Sun-Times, 113
Chincholles, Charles, 19
Chopin, Dan, 110
Chorus Line, A, 102
Churchill, Winston, 56, 71, 86, 87, 92, 104, 106, 115, 123, 126, 133, 134
Ciardi, John, 130, 143
Cicero, 107
Cioran, E.M., 107
Clancy, Tom, 39
Clark, Blake, 123
Clark, Frank A., 10
Clarke, Arthur C., 79, 130
Clemenceau, Georges, 123
Clethan, Al, 48
Clisura, Paul, 82
Clopton, Richard, 53
Coakley, Lazlo, 150
Cockburn, Claude, 113
Cocks, Sir Barnett, 147
Cocotas, Peter, 43
Cohen, Felix, 111
Cohen, Irving, 115
Cohn, Bruce, 140
Colegate, Isabel, 73
Coleridge, Samuel Taylor, 71

156

157

158